ANNUALS

ANNUALS

Oceana

AN OCEANA BOOK

This book is produced by
Quantum Publishing Ltd.
6 Blundell Street
London N7 9BH

This edition printed 2007

ISBN 978-1-84573-347-6

QUMPGA2

Manufactured in Singapore by
Universal Graphics Pte. Ltd.
Printed in China by
L. Rex Printing Co. Ltd.

CONTENTS

Introduction

If you want plants that come to flower quickly and provide a long season of blooms, choose annuals. Whatever look you wish to have in your garden can be achieved with annuals. No matter what the weather, location or length of the growing season in your area, you will find a wide choice within the vast range of annuals to beautify your garden. From earliest spring, when pansies' faces pop from flower beds, through the warmer summer months, when marigolds and zinnias blaze with colour, into the crisp days of autumn, when ornamental kale adds new tones to fallen leaves, there are annuals to fit the bill.

Annuals can be used to define areas or to accent them, to unite large sections of the garden, or to make the garden seem bigger or smaller. The tiniest of backyard gardens or balconies high over city streets benefit from containers of colourful flowers. Cut flowers can cheer up the indoors for many months. One of the nicest things about annuals is that you can change the mood they create as often as you change your mind. Go hot one year with beds of red, yellow and orange flowers, and be cool the following year with shades of pastels, blue, violet, white and grey.

Defining an annual

The term annual is applied to garden flowers that complete their life cycle in the span of one growing season. This means they come up in the spring, grow, flower, set seed and then die after the frosts in the autumn.

Annuals are divided into three categories:

Tender annuals are injured by frost and are not planted until all danger of it has passed in spring, growing all summer until killed by the first frost of autumn.

Half-hardy annuals, although they do not tolerate frost, will grow well during cool spring or autumn weather.

Hardy annuals will withstand some frost and are planted either in late autumn or early spring for early colour.

DESIGNING WITH ANNUALS

Use annuals to fill beds, borders and containers with colour. Warm-season annuals such as marigolds, impatiens (*above*) and zinnias are adapted to bloom even during the hottest weather.

When incorporating annuals into the overall design of your garden there are a number of factors you will want to consider: the size and shape of planting beds or borders; locating them to their best advantage; using them with other plants; and choosing plants because of their size, shape and flower and foliage colour.

Flower beds are plantings that are accessible and viewed from all sides. An example is an island bed in the middle of the lawn. The size of a flower bed depends on the size and scale of the property, and should take up no more than one-third of the total area in order to look in pleasing proportion to it. Beds may be formal in design, and if so are usually square, rectangular or some other symmetrical shape with straight sides. Informal beds have curved sides and are rounded or free formed. Which you choose depends on the architecture of the house and the look you want to achieve.

Borders are plantings at the edge of an area and are accessible from three sides at the most. They back onto the house, a wall, a fence or a planting of shrubs or trees. To keep a border in scale and proportion to its surroundings, make it no wider than one-third its length. However, since borders can be worked from only one side, they should be no wider than 1.5 m (5 ft) or it will be difficult to care for them.

The location of beds and borders depends on several factors. Select spots where you can see and enjoy them, both from inside and outside the house. Plantings at the front of the house allow passers-by and visitors to share in the enjoyment of your flowers. Look at existing, permanent features such as the house, trees, driveways, paths and boundary lines between you and your neighbours and work the beds and borders into them so they complement each other best.

Your imagination is the only limiting factor. Plant annuals along garden paths; in front of fences and walls; along the patio, porch or deck; next to garden benches; around the base of trees; under shrubs; at the base of an outside light. They can be used to attract the eye to a focal point in the garden or to camouflage eyesores. If you're new to gardening, start small; you can always add to your plantings in following years if you find you have the time to maintain a larger garden.

Think about using annuals for special effects. Flowering vines are without equal as temporary screens on fences, walls, trellises or arbours. They can be used for privacy or to block out unsightly views such as work areas and refuse storage areas. In newly planted landscapes low-growing annuals can be used as temporary quick covers while the permanent shrubs and ground covers mature.

Patios are especially comfortable when lined with borders of annuals. To increase their livability even more, set containers of annuals in the corners, next to the lounge chairs, or along the steps into the house. When the containers are planted with fragrant flowers, life on the patio will be even more enjoyable. Annuals in hanging baskets can brighten dull walls and create colourful focal points.

You can plant a special cutting

ABOVE: *Calibrochoa* is one of the best foolproof trailing, summer flowering plants for use in hanging baskets. The small petunia-like flowers cover the plants from mid-spring, right up to early autumn. They come in several colours – rose-red, pink, white, yellow, violet, bluish and brownish-orange and a few in-between shades.

LEFT: Caladiums are an excellent shade-loving annual. They can reach a height of 35–40 cm (14–16 in) and should be planted 25 cm (10 in) apart in beds. A foliage plant, there are five varieties with white/green, pink/red, bright pink/rose, white/red and red leaves. Caladiums will add colour and height to shady areas and also work well in containers.

garden or, if space does not allow, use annuals whose blooms make good cut flowers in beds and borders so you will have bouquets to brighten the inside as well as the outside of the house.

Annuals can be used in gardens to create geometric designs or spell out your name. Before planting, lay out the design on the ground. Select annuals with contrasting foliage or flower colour so the design will stand out, and use annuals whose growth habit is compact so the design will remain intact throughout the season. Good choices for annuals to use in such designs are begonias, marigolds, alternanthera, sweet alyssum, phlox and salvia.

The next step in creating the garden is to decide which annuals to plant. First make a list of which plants are suitable for your area by matching the plants' cultural requirements with your climatic conditions of light, temperature, soil condition and water availability. Then decide which of these you want to grow. You can narrow down the list by keeping in mind how plant height, plant shape, type of foliage and flower colours will fit into your garden design. You may also want to think about other considerations such as having flowers for cutting, drying or fragrance.

Whether you plant beds and borders with one type of plant or a mixture of plants depends on several factors. Small beds or narrow borders usually look best with low-growing plants of the same type, as do formal beds. In larger plantings, a variety of heights is more interesting. The tallest plants should be at the back of the border or the centre of the bed, scaling down to low-growing plants at the front or the edges. Against a tall hedge or fence, plant tall annuals, working down to ground-hugging plants in the front.

Plants basically come in three shapes: spiked, rounded and prostrate. A combination of all three shapes within a mixed border or bed is more attractive. This same combination of plant forms is also effective in containers and window boxes too.

The sudden sweet scent of a flower can be a real pleasure. Position scented plants where their fragrance can be best appreciated, such as entryways or sitting areas.

Choice of colour

Colour is a most critical aspect of flower-bed design. It reflects your personality and the personality of your home. A warm scheme made up of red, orange, gold and yellow tones is exciting, happy and cheerful. It draws the eye to the garden and makes it look smaller than it really is. It also makes a garden appear to be warmer than it is. A cool scheme, that is comprised of green, blue, violet and purple, is cooling, soothing and calming. It makes a small garden look larger and is good when used to hide an eyesore since it does not draw attention to itself. It is also the best choice for a quiet garden designed for reading or relaxing.

To help you think more clearly about how colours work with each other you may want to buy a colour wheel at an art supply shop. Those colours that are across the wheel from each other, such as purple and yellow, are complementary colours. These two together create a strong harmony that may be too overpowering for a small garden but could be very striking in a larger space. In split complementary harmony, a colour is used with one of the colours that is on either side of its opposite. In this case you would use yellow with either blue or red. Analagous harmony is a combination that uses three colours in a row on the wheel, such as yellow, gold and orange, or tones of blues and violets.

It is best to start with one colour as predominant and use one or, at the most, two different colours with it. Once you gain experience, you will know if you can add more colours without creating a distracting look.

Monochromatic harmony is a colour scheme that uses only different shades and tones of one colour. To avoid monotony in a monochromatic scheme, introduce different shapes and textures by using different types of plants, such as yellow marigolds, yellow zinnias and yellow gazanias. You could also choose one type and one colour of plant, such as pink impatiens, but plant varieties with differing shades of pink.

Pink is an excellent colour for a

garden that will often be viewed at night, as is white, for light colours look bright at night while dark colours fade into the background after sunset. Pastels in the night garden also add visibility to garden paths. Dark, vivid colours, on the other hand, are best in a garden that will most often be enjoyed in bright sun, for strong sunlight tends to make light colours look washed out and faded.

White can be used on its own or as a buffer for unifying colour in the garden. If you use only one white plant here and another one there, you will end up with a spotty look, so use masses of white between the colours or as a unifying border in front of them. Annuals with white, silver or grey leaves are used in the same way as annuals that have white flowers.

Before making a final colour selection, consider the colour of the house, fence or wall that the bed or border might be seen against and make sure the colours are complementary.

Colour psychology

Employ colour to draw attention towards or away from certain features in your landscape. Remember that colour has a psychological effect. Blue, purple and green, for example, are cool colours that generally tend to look farther away than they really are. It is best to plant them close to porches, patios or decks where they can be seen. They also tone down moods and have a quietening effect. On hot summer days, they may even help moderate temperatures – visually, that is. The opposite effect is achieved with reds, oranges and yellows. These colours enliven and heat things up. Use them to create a lively entry or dramatic focal point. Employ them, too, to draw attention away from unattractive features in the garden. Annuals are the easiest way to start experimenting with colour. Annuals are relatively inexpensive, they provide plenty of colour and, if you don't like the way they look, they're gone with the first frost. Make your choices even simpler and less expensive by planting in containers and moving them around to experiment with colour combinations. Annuals remain useful in the garden as seasonal borders and fill-in's for bare spots.

Colour wheel for garden design

Colour is probably the single most powerful garden design factor. Certain colour combinations have an emotional impact comparable to that of music. Annual flowering plants are the fastest, least expensive and most satisfying way to achieve quantities of garden colour. Almost every colour, shade and tint is available in annuals.

A colour wheel is a diagrammatic way of showing relationships between colours. Colours on the right side of the wheel are warm. Colours on the left side are cool. Colours adjacent to one another are analogous. Opposite colours are complementary.

What is important to gardeners, is how colours clash with or complement one another and the distinction between warm and cool colours. With a wide selection of annual flower colours available, you can change your colour scheme from year to year. Here are some tips for selecting your colour combinations:

- Cool colours are good for close up viewing and warm colours are good for more dramatic displays in your garden.
- To the eye, cool colours tend to recede, and warm colours tend to advance. In practice, this means that cool coloured flowers at the far end of your garden will seem to disappear and warm colours will stand out.
- Planting warm coloured annuals around a warm area will make it seem even hotter. However, if you plant with plenty of cool green, blue, violet and pastel colours, the area won't actually be any cooler, but it will seem so and be a more inviting place.
- Be careful of cool and warm colour combinations. If your garden is primarily cool coloured, a mass of flame orange zinnias in the background would divert attention from the more subtle colours in the foreground and disrupt the harmonious effect.

Other factors to remember

Think beyond flower colour and plant shape when deciding on your list of annuals. Look also for a variety of foliage textures and colours. Some annuals have large, coarse foliage while others have finely cut leaves; a mixture of foliage types is most effective. Most annuals have green leaves, but some have leaves of red, bronze, purple, silver or grey that can be very useful for accents. Foliage colour should also be brought into colour scheme considerations when planning a design.

Annuals do not need to stand alone, although they can. Early-blooming annuals can be combined with spring bulbs, while summer-flowering annuals can be very effective when mixed with perennials and tender bulbs. Use annuals as a border or ground cover in a rose bed, or with shrubs. Annuals can also be combined in herb and vegetable gardens to bring more colour and interest to them.

When time is limited, pick annuals that do not require pinching, are not particularly prone to insect or disease problems, or have flowers that fall cleanly as they die, so that you need not take the time to cut off faded flowers. Those annuals requiring the least amount of maintenance are ageratum, balsam, begonias, browallia, candytuft, celosia, coleus, dianthus, dusty miller, ornamental cabbage and kale, gloriosa daisy, impatiens, kochia, lobelia, monkey flower, nasturtium, nicotiana, phlox, portulaca, salvia, spider flower, sweet alyssum, wishbone flower and vinca.

When choosing annual varieties, you will note that some are sold in what is known as a 'series'. For example, there are 'Super Elfin' impatiens, 'Madness' petunias, 'Boy' marigolds and 'Sprinter' geraniums. Series contain plants of the same growth habit and size but with numerous different colours. Because of this characteristic, it is best when planting different colours of the same annual to choose plants from the same series. They will be more uniform in appearance and therefore more attractive in the garden.

How to grow annuals

Having a beautiful annual garden that you can enjoy and be proud of is not difficult. The most important thing is to start out right; don't take shortcuts to good soil preparation. Once you have this one basic under control, turn your attention to planting out the young plants and the routine maintenance tasks of fertilizing, watering, mulching, weeding, controlling pests and manicuring the garden. If you enjoy doing things for yourself and can make the time for it, starting your own annuals from seed or cuttings can give you a great sense of satisfaction and save you considerable money.

Growing plants from seed

Starting seeds indoors in the winter and early spring is economical, an interesting challenge, and sometimes the only way to grow the specific varieties you want for your garden. Although many annual seeds can be direct-sown into the garden, starting seeds indoors gives them a head start and makes sure of earlier blooming.

You can purchase flats made from compressed peat moss or plastic, or make your own containers from milk cartons, aluminium baking pans or recycled frozen food dishes. A container can be of any size, but should be 6–7.5 cm (2½–3 in) deep to allow for proper root development. The two basic requirements for containers are that they be absolutely clean and that they have drainage holes in the bottom.

Large seeds and seeds of annuals that are difficult to transplant should be sown into individual containers made of plastic or compressed peat moss. In this way the roots will be disturbed very little during transplanting because the entire container can be planted. The roots will grow right through the peat.

The sowing medium can be purchased, such as loam-based mixtures designed for starting seeds. Or you can make it yourself. A good homemade mix is two parts peat moss, one part horticultural sand and three parts

LEFT: Children love to plant sunflowers because their large seeds are easy to handle and quick to germinate. As their name implies, sunflowers do best in full sun, and they tolerate heat and drought.

sterilized soil (either purchased, or sterilized in the oven or steamed in a pot). Never use soil right from the garden for sowing seeds indoors, for it will not drain as well as a prepared soil and may also carry insects and diseases. Most seeds are started indoors six to eight weeks before the outdoor planting date. The exceptions to this are begonia, coleus, dianthus, geranium, impatiens, lobelia, pansy, petunia, salvia and snapdragon, which all need ten to twelve weeks.

Most seeds can be planted as is but a few germinate best when chilled first or soaked or nicked to soften the seed's coating. Place pre-moistened sowing medium into the container to within 0.6 cm (¼ in) of the top. Seedlings are prone to a disease known as damping off. When it occurs, the seedlings suddenly topple over and die. To prevent this, use only containers washed in warm soapy water that contains a few drops of household bleach; rinse well. Use fresh sowing medium; do not reuse compost for starting seeds. Such precautions will minimize the risk of damping off. If you want to be certain your seedlings will be protected, water the medium before sowing with a solution of the fungicide benomyl or thiram and let the container drain for an hour or two before planting so it will not be too wet.

It will be easier to handle seedlings if seeds are sown in rows, but this will be difficult for small seeds, that can be scattered over the surface of the medium. Except for those seeds that require light to germinate and very fine seeds, cover the seeds with enough moistened medium so that they are just covered. Seeds that require light to germinate and very fine seeds should not be covered, but rather should be pressed into the medium with your hand or with a fine spray of water.

After the seeds are sown, place the entire container into a clear plastic bag. Put the container in good light but not full sun and give it bottom heat to increase germination. You can use heating cables purchased at garden centres specifically for providing bottom heat, or you can place the container in a warm spot, such as on the top of the refrigerator.

Some fine seeds need darkness to germinate. Since fine seeds should not be covered with potting soil, place the container into a black plastic bag until germination occurs.

Until the seeds germinate, they should need no care. If excessive moisture accumulates on the inside of the bag, open it and let the medium dry out slightly. After the seeds have germinated, remove the plastic bag and place the containers in a sunny window or greenhouse, or under fluorescent lights, or special grow lights that are turned on for 12 to 16 hours a day. Once the seedlings have developed two sets of leaves, they should be thinned out or transplanted into individual containers so their roots have enough room to grow.

During the growing period, keep the containers well watered but not soggy. Bottom watering is best as it will not dislodge young seedlings and their tiny roots. Start fertilizing weekly with a weak solution (quarter-strength) of liquid fertilizer.

About one week before the outdoor planting date, start moving the plants outside during the day, returning them indoors at night, to 'harden off' the seedlings and get them used to the outdoor environment.

Many seeds may be started outdoors in the beds and borders where they are to grow; some are actually best started this way because they do not like to be transplanted. Soil should be prepared first (read the section on soil), and the seeds sown according to package directions. After sowing seeds, firm the soil around them with your fingers. Seed beds must be kept constantly moist until the seeds have germinated. Since emerging weeds can often be confused with seedlings, it is best to plant seeds in neat rows and mark them carefully. Weed the bed regularly since fast-growing weeds can rob tender young plants of light, water and nourishment. Once the seeds are growing and have developed two sets of leaves, they should be thinned out and transplanted to the desired part of the garden.

Growing from cuttings

Some annuals can be grown from stem cuttings instead of or in addition to seeds – for example, impatiens, New Guinea impatiens, geraniums, ivy geraniums and coleus. Cuttings can be taken in autumn to grow these plants indoors over the winter, or from indoor grown plants to create new plants for the outdoor garden.

To root a stem cutting, cut a piece of stem that contains at least four and preferably six to eight leaves. Remove the lower two leaves and insert the leafless section of the stem into a container with pre-moistened soilless medium. Application of rooting hormone to the bottom tip of the cutting will aid in and speed up rooting.

After the cutting is in place, place the container in a clear plastic bag and set it in a warm spot with good light but not direct sun. Test the cutting for rooting after several weeks by gently tugging on the stem. If it offers resistance, roots have formed and the plastic bag can be removed. If the stem moves freely, rooting has not yet occurred. Return the cutting to the plastic bag and try again after several weeks.

Once the cutting is rooted, it can be planted into the garden or grown indoors on a sunny windowsill.

Some of the best annuals for stem cuttings are impatiens, geraniums, begonias (*above*), sweet-potato vine and coleus.

Getting down to basics

Soil

No matter how well you plan your garden or how high the quality of your plants may be, you will not succeed without a good foundation – a proper soil. Prior to planting, it is necessary to prepare the soil, especially if a flower bed has never before been in the location where planting will be done. After laying out the area, remove all grass, weeds, stones and other debris.

Incorporate organic matter such as peat moss, leaf mould, well-rotted manure or compost at a rate of 25 to 33 per cent of soil volume into the area of the soil where the roots will be growing, that is approximately the top 20 cm (8 in). This means applying 5–6 cm (2–2½ in) of organic matter onto the soil and then digging it in to a depth of 20 cm (8 in).

Organic matter improves soil retention and drainage. It also improves the texture of soil, helping to make it lighter and 'fluffier' (which means there is more air in it), which is good for plant roots that need to breathe, and good for gardeners who find nice loamy soil easier to work. If your soil is sandy or has a lot of clay in it, more organic matter may improve its texture.

Heavy clay soil can also be improved with the addition of horticultural sand or grit. Gypsum, or calcium sulphate, can be worked into heavy soils as well. It is a good source of calcium and does not change the pH of the soil.

Flower-beds and borders should not be worked in early spring when the soil is still wet or the soil texture will be ruined. Beds and borders can be worked the previous autumn, or in spring just prior to planting. To test the soil to see if it is ready to be worked, take a handful of it and squeeze it. If it sticks together, it is still too wet. Wait a few days and try again. When the soil is ready to be worked, the ball of soil will crumble in your hand.

If you have sufficient organic matter, especially well-rotted manure or good compost worked into your soil each year, and if your soil pH is not too alkaline nor too acid (see page 22), it should be sufficiently fertile for almost all annuals. If, however, the organic matter available to you is peat moss or leaf mould (neither of which contain many nutrients), or your soil is sandy and therefore drains quickly, washing soil nutrients away, you may need to use some fertilizer.

Fertilizers

Gardeners need to be able to recognize the differences between a healthy, vigorous plant and one that is lacking in one or more nutrients. There are a few basic problems to look for. Is there a reasonable amount of new growth? Is the foliage full sized? Is the foliage colour normal? Are the flowers as numerous as expected? Are the flowers full sized? Are the flowers a colour that is typical? Are there insects or diseases present? For example, bicolour petunias will sometimes change the width of the white picotee band on the flower. If the white area expands then temperatures are high, the soil is too dry, or the soil nutrients are low.

The three main plant nutrients are nitrogen, phosphorous and potassium. These are required in the largest amount and are represented by the three number ratio on fertilizer packages. These three numbers represent the percentage of each nutrient by product weight. Nitrogen (N) is the first number and is essential for all stages of plant growth. It is rapidly depleted from the soil because of its soluble nature. Nitrogen, through the application of manure, liquid fertilizer or granular amendments should be well-monitored. Plants that are deficient in nitrogen will be smaller, slow-growing and have paler leaves. As the deficiency continues the lower leaves will turn yellow and fall. Sandy soils are particularly problematic with nitrogen deficiency. An excess of nitrogen can also cause problems. Too much nitrogen can lead to lush, succulent growth at the expense of flowers. Plants could be more susceptible to pests and diseases because of this soft growth.

Many different types of fertilizers are available for use in annual beds. Water-soluble fertilizers will produce the fastest response in plants. They can be applied so that they are absorbed as a foliar feed in addition to a drench. A wide selection of water-soluble fertilizers can be used to customize your fertilizer programme. Many of these have been developed for the commercial greenhouse industry, but are acceptable for outdoor use. The most popular formulations for use on annuals are 10–52–10 (for plant establishment), 15–30–15 (for flowering and fruiting) and 20–20–20 (for general growth). The water-soluble fertilizers can be mixed in a watering can for small applications or fed through a hose using a siphon injector. It could be very inefficient to fertilize large annual beds with a liquid fertilizer. A granular or soil amendment might be a better solution. Do not apply liquid fertilizers to plants growing in dry soils. Irrigate plants first. The salts in the fertilizer could damage plant roots and burning might occur.

Slow release fertilizers are valuable, particularly in hanging baskets or planters. In this situation, frequent watering will leach out nitrogen and other nutrients from liquid fertilizing. Slow release fertilizers use soil temperature to trigger the speed of fertilizer release which usually is over 3–4 months.

Granular fertilizers are easy to add to annuals' beds before, during or after planting. Do not use turf fertilizers in the flower beds. Turf fertilizers have been formulated for an entirely different purpose.

Fertilizers for annuals (and perennials) in granular form will usually be found with a 10–10–10 or 7–7–7 ratio. This well-balanced fertilizer is ideal for use if no deficiency problems are present. It will be faster acting than the slow-release fertilizer and should be watered into the soil. Try to keep solid fertilizers off the foliage of annuals. Damage may occur, particularly if the foliage is wet.

Soil amendments such as compost, manure, bone meal, blood meal and other natural products can also be used to add nutrients to the soil. Each will have a different fertilizer analysis so pick the one that is best suited to your needs. These should be used in combination with other forms of fertilizer. Annuals are expected to grow, flower fast and keep on flowering throughout the season. It is critical that their fertilizer needs are met immediately. Any check in growth will delay the much anticipated flower show.

With all fertilizers, follow the recommended rates on the package. Increasing the rates could have disastrous consequences. Too much fertilizer is not a good thing.

Your soil's pH

Soils for most annuals should be slightly acid to neutral with a pH of 6.0 to 7.0. A few plants like azalea, heather, and rhododendron (*right*) grow best in soils that are a bit more acid (have a lower pH), but an acidic soil will not make most plants happy, and it also has a tendency to bind up certain soil nutrients, making them unavailable to plants. Earthworms, that aerate soil as they tunnel about and fertilize it with their excrement, don't like acidic soil either.

If you are not sure of the pH of your soil, test it yourself with a soil test kit; it is simple, inexpensive, and can be purchased at garden centres. If the pH test results show that your soil is not within the normal range, there are some things you can do to adjust the soil's pH.

For soil that is too acidic, that is more often the problem than a soil that is too alkaline, you can apply limestone; it will not burn plants and it contains magnesium, an element beneficial for plant growth. Do not dig limestone into the soil. Spread it over the soil after it has been dug up, preferably before a rain; alternatively you can water it well. Alkaline soil is not easy to make more neutral; work lots of peat moss (that is naturally acidic) into it annually, or add sulphate of ammonia according to label directions.

PURCHASING PLANTS

You have three choices when it comes to buying annuals.

- Buy seeds and sow them directly where the plants are to grow and bloom.

- Buy seeds and start them indoors and then transplant the seedlings to the garden later.

- Buy transplants of varying sizes (from small plants in six-packs to larger ones in gallon cans). Most often, buying transplants from local nurseries is the easiest approach. You can also buy transplants of annuals by mail and, in doing so, enjoy more choice.

If you buy plants, look for deep green, healthy plants that are neither too compact nor too spindly. Although it is tempting to select plants that are in bloom, it is better if they are not (except for African marigolds, that must be in bud or blooming when planted or they will not bloom until late summer). Most annuals will come into full bloom faster in the garden if they are not in bloom when planted.

If it's not possible for you to plant them right away, keep them in a lightly-shaded spot and be sure to water them as needed, that will probably be every day. Just prior to planting, annual bedding plants should be well watered, as should the soil in the bed or border.

Many plants that bloom easily from seed can reseed themselves and come back year after year on their own. Most annual wild flowers reproduce themselves this way. Towards the end of the season, let annuals such as alyssum, calendula, cosmos, forget-me-nots, marigolds, pansies and violas, sunflowers, vinca and zinnias go to seed for a garden full of volunteers next season.

The advantage of shopping by mail is the large variety available. Virtually any plant that you have ever heard of is available by mail. The disadvantage is that you can't see what you're buying. You are often spending top money for baby plants and have the added cost of shipping. Try placing a small order the first time you shop with a mail order source. This will reduce the risk of receiving small or poor quality plants. Also be aware that mail order companies sometimes ship substitutes in the event that the plant you ordered is out of stock. Be sure to make the retailer know if this is not acceptable to you. Remember, that it's very important to unpack your order immediately upon its arrival.

The best advice when purchasing annuals is to visit as many of the local nurseries and garden centres in your area and take your time shopping. Shop early and often for the best selection and quality. You will soon know which establishments offer the best deals or variety of plants. Collect seed and plant catalogues. They are a wealth of information and may offer a plant that is not available locally.

Planting

Before you plant the annual garden, it is a good idea to lay the plan of your beds and borders out on paper. The best way to do this is with graph paper which makes it easy to draw to scale. A plan of your garden will allow you to decide the shape and size of the borders and beds in advance. In addition, you will also have a pretty good idea of how many plants you will need to grow or buy. You can transfer the plan from the paper to the garden by translating the scale you've chosen (that is one square on the paper equals 30 cm/1 ft) and then measuring off distances with a tape measure then laying it out with sticks and string.

Do not jump the gun on planting time! Tender annuals cannot be planted until all danger of frost has passed. Half-hardy annuals can be safely planted if nights are still cool as long as there will be no more frost. Hardy annuals can be planted in early spring as soon as the soil can be worked.

When planting time comes, use the spacing guidelines already mentioned, and lift the plant from the container carefully, keeping the root ball intact to avoid damage. The best way to do this is to either gently squeeze or push up the bottom of the container if it is pliable enough, or turn the container upside down and let the plant fall into your hand. If the plant does not slide out easily, tap the bottom of the container with a trowel. If the root ball is moist, as it should be, it should slip out easily without being disturbed.

Occasionally, plants are grown in containers that do not have individual cells. Separate the plants gently by hand or with a knife just prior to planting them so the roots do not dry out. Sometimes plants are grown in individual peat moss pots. To plant these, rip off a layer on the outside of the pot and put the plant and the pot into the ground. Be sure the top of the pot is below the soil level after planting or it will act as a wick and draw water away from the plant's roots.

If roots are extremely compacted, loosen them gently before planting so the plants will grow better. Dig a hole slightly larger than the root ball, set the plant in place at the same level at which it was growing, and carefully firm the soil around the roots. Water well after planting and then frequently until plants are established and new growth has started. An application of liquid fertilizer high in phosphorous is beneficial at this time to encourage root growth.

It is best to plant on a cloudy or overcast day, or late in the afternoon to reduce transplanting shock. Petunias are the most notable exception to this rule, tolerating planting even on hot and sunny days.

To reduce garden maintenance, use one of the commercially available pre-emergent herbicides labelled for ornamental use. These prevent weed seeds from germinating. Such preparation will lessen your weeding chores later in the summer. Since these herbicides usually work best if they are not disturbed after application, it is advisable to apply them to the soil right after planting and water them in as required.

How to make compost

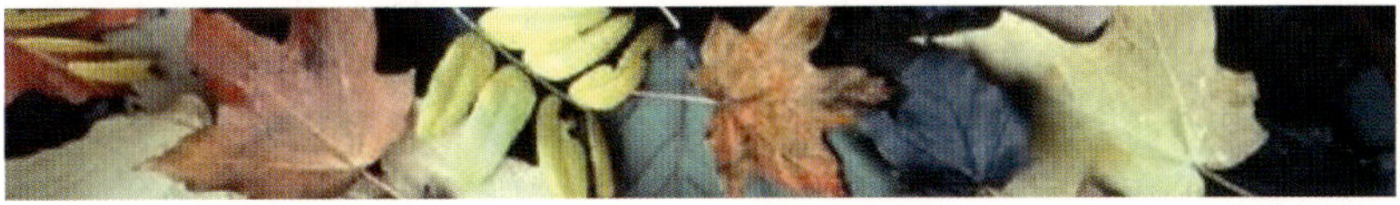

A compost heap is a recycling centre in your own garden. It takes leaves and other plant debris, grass clippings, fruit and vegetable scraps and any other such matter you might have around and, with a little help from you and Mother Nature, transforms them into the best soil additive and plant food there is.

The difference between a well-decomposing pile of organic matter and a heap of rotting debris is plentiful air, warmth, moisture and the proper balance between materials rich in nitrogen and those rich in carbon.

The pile should be at least 1 m (3 ft) high and 1 m (3 ft) wide, and made up of layers of various organic matter. For example, it might start with a layer of plant debris and leaves (no diseased plants or roots of perennial weeds like bindweed or couch grass), then some grass clippings, a layer of kitchen waste (no meats or fats), then a sprinkling of soil and then a repetition of such layers. Cover the whole with another sprinkling of soil, and water it until the pile is moist but not soggy.

Let it stand for a week and then turn the pile with a pitch fork so that all the layers get mixed up and it is aerated. Turn again every two weeks and water if necessary. If the material you added to the pile was in relatively small pieces and the temperature outdoors is warm, you should have finished compost in about three months.

To ensure a well-decomposed compost – especially if your supply of nitrogen-rich plant matter like grass clippings and green leaves is not abundant – you can add blood meal or a commercial 'compost-making enzyme' to the pile as you layer it. If you have access to animal manure, add thin layers of it between thicker layers of plant matter as you make your heap, and let the pile stand for a year before you use it in the garden to make sure the manure is fully decomposed.

Growing the annual garden

The first steps to a beautiful flower garden, as we have seen, are selection of the right annuals, good soil preparation and proper planting. After that it is up to you and Mother Nature to keep the garden at its peak of colour and beauty.

Use in the landscape

Annual flowers can play an important role in a well-designed landscape. Compared to most perennial landscape plants, annuals require higher levels of both maintenance and water, so plant annual beds in easily-accessible areas and near water sources. Concentrate annuals in beds with other annuals or plants with similar water requirements. Planting annuals randomly throughout the landscape not only increases maintenance, but also lessens the plants' aesthetic impact.

Although annual flowers and plants bring a variety of interesting textures and forms to the landscape, they are most notable for the colour they provide. Plant simple mixtures of colour.

Annuals are an excellent way to draw attention to building and home entrances, paths and outdoor living spaces, and to provide homeowners and visitors with pleasing 'up-close' visual and fragrant experiences. Again, it is important to be selective in placing annuals so their ability to draw attention is not diluted.

Plant height is another important design consideration. Typically, a flower border has the tallest plants in the back, medium height plants in the middle and short plants in the front. An island planting places the tallest plants in the middle of the bed, surrounded by plants of decreasing heights.

Watering

Deep, infrequent watering is better than frequent, light applications of water, as the former encourages deep root growth which results in healthier plants. Most annuals need to be watered about as often as the lawn does. When dry soil is called for, allow the top 2.5 cm (1 in) of soil to become dry before re-

LEFT: Overwatering causes periwinkles to die from fungal disease. Once established they do not want any extra water.

watering. When moist soil is required, never let the surface of the soil dry out. Annuals with average water requirements can be watered when the soil surface becomes dry.

If possible, do not let the foliage become wet during watering, as this can spread disease. Soaker hoses that are porous, so that water slowly leaks out onto the ground, or other methods of ground watering are the best way to achieve this. However, if overhead sprinklers must be used, you should water those annuals that are disease prone (zinnias and calendula in particular) as early as possible in the day so that the foliage will dry out before the night. When growing annuals for cut flowers, do not water them overhead if at all possible to prevent water damage to the blooms.

Where rainfall is low and water supplies are short, choose a drought-resistant annual such as portulaca, celosia, cosmos, sunflower, candytuft, dusty miller, gazania, spider flower, sweet alyssum or vinca (periwinkle).

Mulching

After your annuals are planted, adding a 5–7.5 cm (2–3 in) layer of mulch will not only make the garden more attractive, it will also keep weeds down and conserve soil moisture. The best mulches are organic in nature, and include bark chips, pine needles, shredded leaves, peat moss or hulls of some kind. The following year, the mulch can be incorporated into the soil before planting, enriching it. Additional mulch can be added each spring, resulting in better soil structure and therefore better growth as years pass.

If the summers in your region are hot, annuals that require cool soil should be mulched immediately after planting, as this will keep the soil cool in the summer. Annuals that like warm soil should not be mulched until the weather and the soil has warmed up. Black plastic mulch can be used to keep the soil warm while reducing weeds. Be sure there are enough holes in the plastic for water to penetrate the soil below.

ABOVE: Tall dahlias may need to be staked to encourage them to stand upright. Always drive stakes at planting time so that the roots are not accidentally damaged later on.

Staking and tying

Most annuals do not need to be staked, but now and then a few of them do, because they are too heavy or too tall to stand up by themselves. Use a sturdy stake of wood or bamboo and tie the plant to it loosely with a twist tie or string. Don't tie too tightly or the stem will be pinched or damaged. Large bushy plants may need three or four stakes around the outside of the plant to keep them upright and compact. Large plants can also be staked with large wire cones, often called tomato cages, or with similar devices.

Some vines will cling on their own, but others need help. Tie vines loosely to their supports without tying so tight as to damage the stems. Vines can also be woven through trellises and fences made of chicken wire or similar material.

WEEDING

Weeding is more than removing unwanted plants that make flower beds and borders unattractive. Weeds compete with annuals for water, light and nutrients, and are breeding grounds for insects and diseases. Weeds will appear, even if you use mulch. Be sure to remove them as soon as possible. Remove weeds carefully, especially when the annuals are young, so you do not disturb the annuals' roots. Weeds can be pulled by hand or, when the annuals are mature, worked out with a hoe.

SELF-SOWING

Some annuals, particularly impatiens, portulaca, salvia and nicotiana, will self-sow, or reseed themselves, from one year to the next, or sometimes during the same growing season. The seedlings of hybrid plants will not be identical to the parent and will often be less vigorous. It is best to remove these and replant all flower-beds and borders with new annuals each year for maximum effect. Seeds of non-hybrid plants can be left to grow if you wish, and the annuals will act as though they were perennials. However, in areas with short growing seasons, these seedlings may never grow large enough to be showy, so you can't rely on this and will need to replant.

PINCHING AND PRUNING

A few annuals, primarily petunias, snapdragons and pansies, may need to be pinched back after planting or after the first flush of bloom to keep them compact and freely flowering. As new and more compact hybrids are created, this is becoming less important. Sweet alyssum, candytuft, phlox and lobelia may tend to sprawl and encroach on paths, the lawn or other flowers. They can be headed back with hedge clippers if this occurs. This shearing will also encourage heavier blooming. When flowers are taken from annuals as they fade or when cut for cut flowers, the plants are in effect being pruned.

Dead-heading

Some annuals, chiefly begonias, impatiens, coleus, alyssum, ageratum, lobelia, vinca and salvia, require little additional care. Their flowers fall cleanly from the plant after fading and do not need to be manually removed. Others, such as marigolds, geraniums, zinnias, calendula and dahlias, will need to have their faded flowers removed. This is known as dead-heading and is necessary to keep the plants, attractive in full bloom, from going to seed, and to prevent disease. Dead-heading can be done with pruning shears or sometimes with the fingers.

Annual phlox (*right*) is tricky to dead-head because there is little difference in look between a forming flower bud and a finished seed head. Canna (*below*) is tricky because if the spent flower is pruned too far down the stem then the next flower bud is removed too. During dead-heading, be wary of stinging insects that like to frequent flowers. Grabbing a canna bloom to dead-head it and finding an angry bee is not a pleasant experience.

Care in the Autumn

In the autumn, after frost has blackened the tops of annual plants, they should be removed so the beds are not unsightly through the winter. Removal of plants also eliminates sites where insects and diseases can shelter during winter. Dig or pull them out and put them on the compost pile, if the plants are not diseased or infected with insects.

INSECT AND DISEASE CONTROL

Annuals can be relatively trouble-free provided they receive the proper care. Here are the most common problems that may develop.

INSECTS

APHIDS These are very small, winged insects that are light green, brown or cream in colour; the light green aphids are the most common on annuals. Their presence is usually noticeable by the honey-dew they exude as they suck sap. This sticky substance attracts ants and sometimes encourages a sooty mould to grow on it. A heavy infestation can stunt or deform plant growth and prevent flowers from developing properly.

If not many plants are infested, the aphids can often be washed off quite easily with a solution of soap and water. Organic sprays include derris, pyrethrum and quassia. Diazinon, malathion and sevin are effective chemical insecticides. Ladybirds, natural predators of aphids, should be encouraged.

MEALY BUGS These cottony white insects can be found on the undersides of leaves and on stems. For small infestations wipe off with a damp cloth. Pull out and burn badly infested plants. Diazinon or malathion will only help if the affected areas are sprayed heavily.

EARWIGS Recognizable for their large pinchers, earwigs hide inside flowers and come out to eat ragged holes in the petals and leaves. Since they like to hide, trap them in inverted flower pots under which you have placed dry leaves, straw or crumpled newspaper. Alternatively, spray plants with diazinon, malathion or sevin.

LEFT: Aphids are the most common cause of damage to annuals.

SLUGS AND SNAILS Slugs and snails eat green leaves, especially those of young plants, often weakening them so much that they die. Remove any moist or soft mulch around plants and replace with a mulch of sand or another rough, dry mulch.

Sink saucers in the soil around susceptible plants and keep filled with beer as it evaporates. Remember to replace beer that becomes diluted with rainwater; remove dead slugs that go in for a drink but can't climb out again.

THRIPS These are tiny black insects that suck sap from leaves and flowers, leaving silver streaks in their paths. They can wither the edges of flowers and distort them. They are most prevalent during hot, dry weather. Spray with the organic insecticide derris, or chemical sprays and dusts like diazinon, malathion or nicotine.

Recognizing common insects

ABOVE: Earwigs produce tiny holes in leaves and stems.

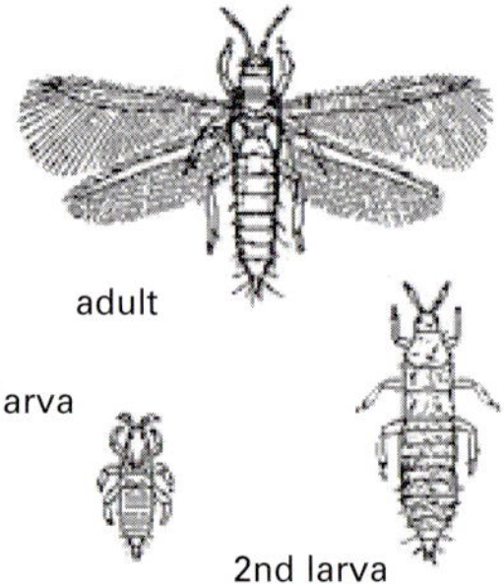

ABOVE: Thrips leave foliage and flowers streaked and spotted.

ABOVE: Aphids attack the soft tissue of the plant.

LEFT: Slugs are attracted to water around the plant base.

CATERPILLARS Larvae from several kinds of moths and butterflies can eat buds and foliage. Insects sometimes roll themselves in leaves in spring. Spray with the organic insecticide derris, pick off the infested shoots by hand, or use a chemical spray of diazinon or sevin.

Diseases

DAMPING OFF This is any one of a number of diseases that causes a fungus to rot seedlings at the soil level; they topple over and die. Prevention is best: use a sterile sowing medium; clean all containers and tools with soap and water containing a few drops of household bleach, then rinse well. Don't sow seeds too thickly and be careful not to overwater. For extra protection, treat the soil before sowing with a fungicide like thiram or benomyl. Should the condition exist, you may be able to control it by watering with captan or thiram.

POWDERY MILDEW Affected plants will be coated with a fine white or grey powder and they will be stunted. Prevention is best: plant those plants most susceptible to it, like chrysanthemum, delphinium and Michaelmas daisy, in an open area not too close together; do not let the plants get too dry by mulching them and watering regularly in dry times. Remove diseased plants promptly.

RUST A variety of fungi may cause yellow and green mottlings on the upper surfaces of leaves and orange or brown spots on the undersides. Plant disease-resistant cultivars of those plants most affected, like antirrhinum, chrysanthemum, hollyhock and Sweet William. Keep plants healthy by watering and fertilizing as needed. Remove and burn infested plants.

VIRUS Since there are several viruses that can affect plants, the symptoms vary, but generally affected plants are stunted with deformed, mottled leaves. Since there is no cure or real control, prevent by buying virus-resistant cultivars and keep plants healthy. Remove and burn infested plants promptly.

Growing annuals in containers

Whether you live in a flat where you haven't much room, or on a country estate with acres of garden, containers have their place. Container gardening gives you the luxury of having colours, shapes, sizes and textures just where you want them. Start imagining how that certain spot would look with a splash of colour or with a pot of cascading cool green foliage. Choices for containers are almost endless. Plants will grow in most anything that will hold soil and has good drainage, so don't overlook that old coal scuttle with holes in the bottom or that wooden crate sitting in your garage. Let your imagination be your guide. You want your container to hold enough soil for your plants to get what they need. Remember, if a pot is too big, plants will often spend all their efforts growing roots instead of top growth.

If the container does not have drainage holes and none can be made, a thick layer of small stones must be placed in the bottom of the planter to prevent water-logging of the roots.

Containers

It doesn't take much looking to find an amazing selection of containers available in various shapes, sizes and materials, all of them with their merits. Just keep in mind that growing in a container is easy, but it is not nature's way. Your container will need to hold sufficient soil to support your annuals throughout the growing season. Generally, the larger the container, the happier your plants will be and the more freedom you will have to create mixed plantings. Larger containers are also more stable against wind and pets. The most important consideration beyond size is aesthetics – choose containers that complement the surroundings and the plants.

- Clay has weight for stability, breathes, is affordable, and provides traditional style and beauty. It should be stored inside for the winter, and with care, it can last decades.
- Plastic containers come in hundreds of shapes, colours and

sizes. It is a lightweight choice for ease in moving and storing. It is also inexpensive and holds moisture longer than most other containers. Most plastic pots can stay outdoors all year if needed, but will last longer if stored indoors. Depending on the type of plastic, these pots usually last several years.

- Wood adds its own unique style to containers and is medium weight, porous and moderately expensive. Wood containers can stay outdoors and, if made of rot-resistant timber, can last ten or more years.

- Concrete containers are heavy, come in a variety of finishes and styles, and are usually an affordable alternative for large pots. Concrete can stay out all year and lasts for decades.

LEFT: Garden geraniums thrive in containers, and are well suited to hanging baskets.

A–Z ENCYCLOPEDIA OF PLANTS

Abelmoschus moschatus • *Muskmallow*

DESCRIPTION

One of about 15 species in the genus, and a member of the mallow (Malvaceae) family, this species is found from tropical Asia to northern Australia. Its stem and leaves bear bristly hairs and its leaf lobes are triangular. While the species is variable, and bears white, pink or yellow flowers, with a dark eye, the Pacific Series comprises scarlet- and pink-flowered cultivars that bloom in summer.

The abundant seeds yield the musky perfume, ambrette. Propagation is by basal cuttings or seed sown as soon as the weather is warm enough in late spring.

Species, variety or cultivar:
Pacific Series

Other common names:
Muskmallow

Height and spread:
1.8 x 75 cm (6 x 30 in)

Blooming period:
Summer

Soil type:
Well-drained soil, fertilized in summer

Sun or Shade:
Likes a sunny position sheltered from strong winds

Hardiness:
Minimum temp –1°C (30°F)

Actinotus helianthi • *Flannel Flower*

Description

This Australian species is somewhat woody and short-lived, and is found on the shallow, sandy, acid soils of the Sydney region. It also occurs on deep coastal sand dunes further north of Sydney, in low sclerophyllous heaths, shrublands, and woodlands.

Creamy white to grey, felty bracts are sometimes green-tipped, and flowerheads are up to 10 cm (4 in) in diameter. Can be propagated from cuttings and seeds, and current breeding and selecting programmes are producing cultivars suitable for various horticultural purposes, including cut flowers for export.

Species, variety or cultivar:
–

Other common names:
Flannel Flower

Height and spread:
150 x 100 cm (60 x 40 in)

Blooming period:
Late winter through to summer

Soil type:
Sandy, acid soil

Sun or Shade:
Enjoys full sun

Hardiness:
Minimum temp –12°C (10°F)

Adonis annua • *Pheasant's Eye*

Description

Native from southern Europe to south-western Asia, this species has also naturalized in the UK and northern Europe. With fine ferny foliage on upright stems, and flowers that are blood red in colour with a black base, this is an ideal species for the rock garden, or the front of borders.

A member of the buttercup (Ranunculaceae) family, the genus was named after the beautiful youth of Greek mythology who was killed by a wild boar and changed into a flower by Aphrodite.

Species, variety or cultivar:
–

Other common names:
Pheasant's Eye

Height and spread:
40 x 30 cm (16 x 12 in)

Blooming period:
Summer

Soil type:
Moist but well-drained soil

Sun or Shade:
Likes a sunny site

Hardiness:
Minimum temp –40°C (–40°F)

Ageratum houstonianum • *Floss Flower*

Description

A member of the daisy (Asteraceae) family, the genus Ageratum gets its name from the Greek *a* (without) and *geras* (age), which refers to the long-lasting qualities of the flowers. The genus is best known for the annual bedding species, *A. houstonianum*.

Native to Central America and the West Indies, this species has pointed oval to poplar-shaped, downy, tooth-edged, dull green leaves to nearly 10 cm (4 in) long. A popular cultivar is 'Azure Pearl' which has large open heads of mid-blue flowers.

Species, variety or cultivar:
'Azure Pearl'

Other common names:
Floss Flower

Height and spread:
75 x 50 cm (30 x 20 in)

Blooming period:
Summer

Soil type:
Gritty well-drained soil that remains moist during the flowering season

Sun or Shade:
Prefers full sun

Hardiness:
Minimum temp –1°C (30°F)

Ageratum houstonianum • *Floss Flower*

Species, variety or cultivar:
Hawaii Series 'Hawaii Royal'
Other common names:
Floss Flower
Height and spread:
50 x 50 cm (20 x 20 in)
Blooming period:
Summer
Soil type:
Gritty well-drained soil that remains moist during the flowering season
Sun or Shade:
Prefers full sun
Hardiness:
Minimum temp –1°C (30°F)

Description

Ageratum is characterized by flowerheads in which the ray florets are tubular filaments rather than petal-like, creating an attractive feathery effect. The species *A. houstonianum* has several seedling strains of uniform size, but varying flower, and one of the best of these is the Hawaii Series. A great example is 'Hawaii Royal' which gives a showy display of striking dark pink flowers.

Alcea rosea • *Hollyhock*

DESCRIPTION

Widely cultivated and naturalized, this species is thought to have originated from Turkey or Asia. Rounded leaves have three to seven lobes and the flowers grow to 10 cm (4 in) across. 'Nigra' has very dark maroon single flowers.

Rust can be a problem for this genus and it is best to renew plants each year. Plants on exposed sites should be staked and watered in dry spells. Propagate from seed sown in late summer or early spring.

Species, variety or cultivar:
'Nigra'

Other common names:
Hollyhock

Height and spread:
2.4 x 0.9 m (8 x 3 ft)

Blooming period:
Spring through summer

Soil type:
Rich soil, moist but well drained

Sun or Shade:
Enjoys a sunny position

Hardiness:
Minimum temp –40°C (–40°F)

Althea officinalis • *Marsh Mallow*

Species, variety or cultivar:
–

Other common names:
Marsh Mallow, White Mallow

Height and spread:
2 x 1.2 m (7 x 4 ft.)

Blooming period:
Summer

Soil type:
Rich moist soil

Sun or Shade:
Prefers a sunny position

Hardiness:
Minimum temp –40°C (–40°F)

Description

Originally from Europe, and now naturalized in the USA, this species grows in moist or marshy ground at low altitudes. It is a rather lax plant with hairy, greyish, three to five lobed leaves. The small flowers are pale pink or white with purplish red tubes of fused stamens, borne in racemes or panicles in summer.

Ideal for 'wild' gardens, and growing best in rich moist soil in a sunny position, this species is propagated by division or from seed in spring. The popular confectionery marshmallow was originally made from the roots of this plant.

Alyssum montanum • *Madwort*

DESCRIPTION

This is a European alpine species, spreading, and usually prostrate. It has downy pale grey leaves in rosettes and sprays of small, honey-scented, yellow flowers with notched petals. 'Berggold' (also known as 'Mountain Gold') is a popular low spreading cultivar with golden yellow flowers that appear in summer.

An ideal plant for rockeries, stone walls or cascading over banks, they are drought tolerant once established, but benefit from occasional deep watering. The common name comes from an old belief that the plant could cure madness.

Species, variety or cultivar:
'Berggold' or 'Mountain Gold'

Other common names:
Madwort

Height and spread:
20 x 40 cm (8 x 16 in)

Blooming period:
Summer

Soil type:
Light, gritty, well-drained soil

Sun or Shade:
Full sun is ideal

Hardiness:
Minimum temp –23°C (–10°F)

Amaranthus caudatus • *Love-Lies-Bleeding*

Species, variety or cultivar:
'Green Tails'

Other common names:
Love-Lies-Bleeding, Tassel Flower, Velvet Flower

Height and spread:
120 x 60 cm (48 x 24 in)

Blooming period:
Summer

Soil type:
Easily grown in well-drained fertile soil

Sun or Shade:
Enjoys full sun

Hardiness:
Minimum temp – 12°C (10°F)

Description

Native to Peru, Africa and India, this annual species has dull green leaves, as well as drooping crimson-purple tassels that grow up to 30 cm (12 in) long in summer. The cultivar 'Green Tails' differs in having long greenish yellow tassels.

Does best if protected from strong wind. In cooler climates sow seed under glass in early spring and plant out after danger of frosts has passed. In warmer areas seed can be sown outdoors later in the season.

Amaranthus tricolor • *Chinese Spinach*

DESCRIPTION

From Asia and Africa, this bushy annual species is grown as a leaf vegetable or, in varieties that have colourful foliage, for its ornamental value. Flower spikes are green or red and appear in summer. The best known variety with coloured top growth is 'Joseph's Coat', which has stunning red and gold upper leaves, making it an ideal addition to ornamental gardens, as well as popular for floristry.

Species, variety or cultivar:
'Joseph's Coat'

Other common names:
Chinese Spinach, Tampala

Height and spread:
90 x 75 cm (36 x 30 in)

Blooming period:
Summer

Soil type:
Easily grown in well-drained fertile soil

Sun or Shade:
Full sun is best

Hardiness:
Minimum temp –12°C (10°F)

Ammi visnaga • *Bisnaga, Toothpick Weed*

Description

A member of the carrot (Apiaceae) family, this genus is comprised of six species, and is found through much of southern Europe and western Asia. *A. visnaga* has very finely divided pinnate leaves, and in summer produces greenish white flowers that last well when cut and are popular with florists. Inclined to be top-heavy, the species should be staked and sheltered from strong winds.

As the common name suggests, the dried stems are used as toothpicks, and the essential oil has many herbal uses, especially for bronchial troubles. Care should be taken to avoid the sap, which can cause contact dermatitis or other sensitivities.

Species, variety or cultivar:
–

Other common names:
Bisnaga, Toothpick Weed

Height and spread:
0.8 x 1.2 m (32 x 48 in)

Blooming period:
Summer

Soil type:
Free-draining, moist, gritty soil

Sun or Shade:
Prefers a sunny position

Hardiness:
Minimum temp –12°C (10°F)

Anagallis tenella • *Bog Pimpernel*

DESCRIPTION

This primrose (Primulaceae) family genus includes 20 species, found over much of the globe, especially temperate zones. Soft-stemmed, low, spreading plants, these mostly biennials or perennials behave as annuals in cold climates. Small brightly coloured flowers, often in pink, red or blue, form in the leaf axils. Some are considered weeds, but they are not invasive or difficult to control.

A. tenella is a low spreading, native to western Europe, and has paired elliptical leaves on soft stems that strike root as they spread. An attractive cultivar is 'Studland' which has small simple leaves, and fragrant pink flowers that bloom in late spring to early summer in a profuse display that can almost completely obscure the leaves beneath. Best grown in a sunny spot with moist, well-drained soil, this cultivar is easily maintained by pinching to shape, and will not become invasive. Propagation is from seed, base cuttings or by layers.

Species, variety or cultivar:
'Studland'
Other common names:
Bog Pimpernel
Height and spread:
10 x 40 cm (4 x 16 in)
Blooming period:
Late spring to early summer
Soil type:
Moist, well-drained soil
Sun or Shade:
Enjoys a sunny position
Hardiness:
Minimum temp –18°C (0°F)

LEFT AND ABOVE: Despite its common name, this attractive little plant is more often found in wet, marshy conditions in fens, lakeshores and flushes. It is a creeping plant with circular leaves and an abundance of beautiful pale pink flowers. When not flowering it resembles the New Zealand willowherb.

Anchusa azurea • *Bugloss*

Species, variety or cultivar:
'Loddon Royalist'

Other common names:
Alkanet, Bugloss

Height and spread:
1.2 x 0.8 m (48 x 32 in)

Blooming period:
Late spring and summer

Soil type:
Thrives in most conditions, except very poor soil

Sun or Shade:
Likes full to part sun, avoid deep shade

Hardiness:
Minimum temp –40°C (–40°F)

Description

Native to the Mediterranean region and western Asia, this species has bristly red-tinted stems with leaves to 30 cm (12 in) long. A strong grower, with upright stem and simple, pointed, elliptical leaves, this species has heads of small 5-petalled flowers from blue to purple that bloom from late spring through summer. The award winning cultivar 'Loddon Royalist' is compact and bushy, and has large deep blue flowers.

The genus thrives in most conditions except very poor soil, deep shade or drought. A red dye can be extracted, which was once used as a hair colouring, but this is now seldom seen.

Antirrhinum majus • *Snapdragon*

Description

From southwestern Europe, this species has an upright bushy habit, with dark green, elliptical leaves. Flowers appear in spring, in upright racemes, usually pink in the wild, but cultivated in most colours except blue. There are a number of popular seedling series, such as the Sonnet Series, which comes in a variety of colours, including 'Sonnet White'. Snapdragon seed is rich in oil, which in former times was extracted and used like olive oil.

Species, variety or cultivar:
'Sonnet White'

Other common names:
Snapdragon

Height and spread:
150 x 50 cm (60 x 20 in)

Blooming period:
Spring

Soil type:
Fertile, rich, humus-rich soil

Sun or Shade:
Likes full sun, but copes with part shade

Hardiness:
Minimum temp –18°C (0°F)

Aptenia cordifolia • *Heartleaf Iceplant*

Description

A South African genus in the iceplant (Aizoaceae) family, which has just two species – both small, spreading, branching shrubs with fleshy succulent leaves covered in minute protuberance that give the leaves a texture as though they were dusted with fine sugar crystals. *A. cordifolia* is native to the Eastern Cape region of South Africa, has small heart-shaped leaves, and intense magenta flowers.

'Red Apple' is an especially vigorous form, possibly a hybrid, which can be invasive. Surprisingly hardy if kept dry in winter, this little succulent makes a bold splash of colour, its spreading habit making it ideal for rockeries, or as a small-scale ground cover.

Species, variety or cultivar:
'Red Apple'

Other common names:
Heartleaf Iceplant, Hearts and Flowers

Height and spread:
5 x 100 cm (2 x 40 in)

Blooming period:
Summer

Soil type:
Well-drained, gritty soil

Sun or Shade:
Likes sun and partial shade

Hardiness:
Minimum temp –7°C (20°F)

Arctotis acaulis • *African Daisy*

Description

One of about 50 species in this genus from the daisy (Asteraceae) family and found from the southern tip of Africa northward to Angola. A clumping rosette-forming plant, this species has wavy, lobed or toothed leaves to 20 cm (8 in) long, green above and white haired below. The flowerheads are up to 10 cm (4 in) across, with ray florets mainly in yellow, orange or red shades, and disc florets of deep purple.

They thrive in light well-drained soil and full sun. They are drought tolerant but will flower more heavily if watered well in the growing season.

Species, variety or cultivar:
–

Other common names:
African Daisy

Height and spread:
30 x 100 cm (12 x 40 in)

Blooming period:
Summer through to early autumn

Soil type:
Light well-drained soil

Sun or Shade:
Prefers full sun

Hardiness:
Minimum temp –7°C (20°F)

Arctotis venusta • *Blue-eyed African Daisy*

Description

Naturally occurring from Angola and down to the southern tip of Africa, this is a low spreading annual with deeply lobed to almost pinnate, downy, grey-white leaves and heavily ribbed flower stems. Although wild plants usually have deep magenta ray florets and purple-blue disc florets, flowers in cultivation are variably coloured and will bloom for much of the year in the right conditions. Propagate from seed, and plant in light well-drained soil, in full sun.

The name *Arctotis* comes from the Greek and means 'bear's ear', a rather obscure reference to the resemblance of the flower scales to a bear's ear.

Species, variety or cultivar:
Compositae

Other common names:
Blue-eyed African Daisy

Height and spread:
60 x 40 cm (24 x 16 in)

Blooming period:
Summer through to early autumn

Soil type:
Light well-drained soil

Sun or Shade:
Prefers full sun

Hardiness:
Minimum temp –7°C (20°F)

FAR LEFT AND LEFT: Frosty silver foliage shows off the white/blue daisies with blue centres on flowers that bloom all season. Keep pinched for more restrained growth.

Arctotis x hybrida • *African Daisy*

Description

This species has mainly *A. venusta x A. fastuosa* parentage, and is a compact plant, usually with silvery foliage, treated as an annual in cool climates. There are many popular named cultivars and seedling strains, which cover most of the spectrum except blue.

One cultivar that has distinguished itself is the award winning 'Flame', which has attractive bright orange-red flowers that bloom from mid-summer through to early autumn.

Species, variety or cultivar:
'Flame'

Other common names:
African Daisy

Height and spread:
40 x 50 cm (16 x 20 in)

Blooming period:
Summer through to early autumn

Soil type:
Light well-drained soil

Sun or Shade:
Enjoys full sun

Hardiness:
Minimum temp –7°C (20°F)

Asperula orientalis • *Blue Woodruff*

Description

A member of the madder or gardenia (Rubiaceae) family, this annual is found from southern Europe, western Asia, and the Middle East, and has a rangy, upright habit with widely spaced whorls of green leaves to 5 cm (2 in) long. Bristly stems support terminal heads of pleasantly scented lavender-blue, funnel-shaped flowers, which appear from spring through summer.

The neat, compact nature of this species makes it ideal for rockeries and it often self-sows. Plant in a bright position with moist, fertile, well-drained soil and trim after flowering.

Species, variety or cultivar:
–
Other common names:
Blue Woodruff
Height and spread:
30 x 60 cm (12 x 24 in)
Blooming period:
Spring through summer
Soil type:
Moist, fertile, well-drained soil
Sun or Shade:
Likes a bright position
Hardiness:
Minimum temp –12°C (10°F)

Begonia semperflorens

RIGHT: 'Rose Blush'
Begonias can be propagated by seed, leaf cuttings or soft wood cuttings. Some may form many shoots and can be divided. The seed is very fine and may be hard for inexperienced gardeners to work with. Plant seed in a light, well-drained, media kept uniformly moist. Sow the seed thinly and don't cover it. Germination is best when containers are placed 0.3 m (1 ft) below fluorescent lights left on for 24 hours. The seed germinates in two to three weeks at temperatures between 70 and 80 degrees.

Description

Begonias are found naturally occurring through the tropics and subtropics, but are most diverse in the Americas. The Semperflorens Group is comprised of small bushy bedding annuals with bright green or red, glossy, waxy leaves. Flowers are small and usually single. The Ambassador Series is compact with mid-green foliage, and 'Ambassador Blush' has attractive flowers with pink margins fading to white in the centre.

Preferring a bright but not sunny position, this series is ideally suited to cool, fairly moist summers. Roots may rot if the soil becomes too moist, and care should be taken to watch for fungal diseases.

Species, variety or cultivar:
'Ambassador Blush'

Other common names:
–

Height and spread:
30 x 30 cm (12 x 12 in)

Blooming period:
Summer

Soil type:
Fertile, cool, moist, soil rich in humus

Sun or Shade:
Enjoys part to full sun

Hardiness:
Minimum temp –7°C (20°F)

Begonia semperflorens

Description

Found naturally occurring through the tropics and subtropics, Begonias are most diverse in the Americas. The Semperflorens Group is comprised of small bushy bedding annuals with bright green or red, glossy, waxy leaves. Flowers are small and usually single. The Prelude Series is early-blooming with rich green foliage, and 'Prelude White' has elegant single white blooms.

Preferring a bright but not sunny position, the Prelude Series should be planted out at the end of spring. A standard potting compost is ideal. Care should be taken to watch for fungal diseases.

Species, variety or cultivar:
'Prelude White'

Other common names:
–

Height and spread:
30 x 30 cm (12 x 12 in)

Blooming period:
Summer

Soil type:
Fertile, cool, moist, soil rich in humus

Sun or Shade:
Enjoys part to full sun

Hardiness:
Minimum temp –7°C (20°F)

Begonia tuberous group

Description

Members of the Tuberous Group are perhaps the most popular type of begonias. This group grows from large flat tubers, producing short, heavy, succulent stems carrying large, often hairy leaves. They are suitable for indoor or outdoor cultivation, flowering mainly from mid-summer to early frost. There is a huge range of flower types and colours, including many that resemble roses. One such is the cultivar 'Mardi Gras', which is white with dainty pink borders.

Propagation is by dividing the tuber. Plants should be watered well on warm days, taking care that excess water drains away to avoid rotting the roots. Watch for fungal diseases.

Species, variety or cultivar:
'Mardi Gras'

Other common names:
–

Height and spread:
80 x 50 cm (32 x 20 in)

Blooming period:
Summer to autumn

Soil type:
Fertile, cool, moist, soil rich in humus

Sun or Shade:
Enjoys part to full sun

Hardiness:
Minimum temp –12°C (10°F)

Beta vulgaris • *Beet*

DESCRIPTION

The original wild or sea beet is a perennial growing on the seashores of Europe, North Africa and western Asia. All cultivated beets, grown as annuals, are believed to be derived from it, including beetroot, sugar beet, fodder beets such as mangel-wurzel, chard and spinach beet. These are now divided into different groups.

The Cicla Group includes spinach beets, closest to wild beet with a slender green leaf stalk and a flat blade, but also chards or silver beets with larger leaves puckered to varying degree, and a broad, white or coloured, stalk and midrib. 'Bright Yellow' is a spinach beet with yellow stems and green crinkly leaves.

Species, variety or cultivar:
Cicla Group 'Bright Yellow'
Other common names:
Beet
Height and spread:
70 x 70 cm (27 x 27 in)
Blooming period:
–
Soil type:
Light well-drained soil, not too rich
Sun or Shade:
Needs full sun
Hardiness:
Minimum temp –12°C (10°F)

Bidens ferulifolia • *Apache Beggarticks*

DESCRIPTION

This species is found from Arizona (USA) down through Mexico and into Guatemala, and has green ferny foliage. It is one of about 200 species in the *Bidens* genus, which is a member of the daisy (Asteraceae) family. Golden wide-rayed daisies, about 30 cm (1¼ in) across are borne from late summer to autumn.

These plants require little more than a sunny well-drained site with reasonable moisture-retentive soil. Propagate from seed, and plant after frosts in very cold climates. The common name comes from the sticking hooks on the seeds, which help them to become dispersed over wide areas.

Species, variety or cultivar:

–

Other common names:

Apache Beggarticks

Height and spread:

90 x 45 cm (36 x 18 in)

Blooming period:

Late summer to autumn

Soil type:

Reasonable moisture-retentive soil

Sun or Shade:

Likes a sunny site

Hardiness:

Minimum temp –12°C (10°F)

Borago officinalis • *Borage*

Description

Part of the borage (Boraginaceae) family, this genus is made up of just three species from Europe that are generally used in the herb garden or wilder spots where their self-seeding tendencies won't be a problem. *B. officinalis* is a vigorous, self-seeding, upright annual, with leaves that are rough to touch and large open heads of rich blue flowers in summer to 2.5 cm (1 in) across.

Any moisture-retentive soil in sun or half-sun will suit, and propagation is from self-sown seed that will need to be thinned out. The flowers are much loved by bees, and can be eaten in salads. The aromatic young leaves can also be eaten.

Species, variety or cultivar:
–

Other common names:
Borage

Height and spread:
60 x 30 cm (24 x 12 in)

Blooming period:
Summer

Soil type:
Any moisture-retentive soil

Sun or Shade:
Likes both full and part sun

Hardiness:
Minimum temp –29°C (–20°F)

Brachyscome angustifolia • *Stiff Daisy*

Description

Widespread in southeastern Australia, as well as Tasmania, this species is a spreading mound of wiry stems with linear dark green leaves to 5 cm (2 in) long, and pink, blue or purple flowerheads around 2.5 cm (1 in) wide.

The cultivar 'Mauve Delight' has small, bright green leaves, and pretty, daisy-type mauve-pink flowers with yellow centres, borne from spring to early summer. Popular in rock gardens, pots, hanging baskets, on banks and at the front of garden borders, this cultivar will do well in any well-drained soil and in either full or half-sun. Propagation is from seed.

Species, variety or cultivar:
'Mauve Delight'

Other common names:
Stiff Daisy, Grassland Daisy

Height and spread:
38 x 60 cm (15 x 24 in)

Blooming period:
Spring to early summer

Soil type:
Any well-drained soil

Sun or Shade:
Likes both full and part sun

Hardiness:
Minimum temp –7°C (20°F)

Brachyscome iberidifolia • *Swan River Daisy*

Species, variety or cultivar:
'Blue Star'
Other common names:
Swan River Daisy
Height and spread:
30 x 30 cm (12 x 12 in)
Blooming period:
Late spring to early autumn
Soil type:
Any well-drained soil
Sun or Shade:
Likes both full and part sun
Hardiness:
Minimum temp –7°C (20°F)

Description

Native to Western and South Australia, this species is an erect annual daisy with pinnate leaves. The flowers are 2.5 cm (1 in) in diameter in blue, purple or white, and appear from late spring through to early autumn.

The cultivar 'Blue Star' has masses of lightly scented purple-tinted flowers with quilled petals and can be frost tender. Its low spreading habit makes it an ideal choice for rockeries or on banks. It will do well in any well-drained soil in either full or half-sun, and it is reasonably drought tolerant.

Brassica oleracea • *Cauliflower*

Species, variety or cultivar:
Botrytis Group, 'Perfection'
Other common names:
Cauliflower
Height and spread:
40 x 30 cm (16 x 12 in)
Blooming period:
Depends on age of plant and climate
Soil type:
Well-drained moist soil, enriched with well-rotted manure
Sun or Shade:
Needs full sun
Hardiness:
Minimum temp –7°C (20°F)

Description

This species, originating in western Europe is the ancestor of cabbage, broccoli, cauliflower, kale and brussels sprouts. The cultivated types of this species are separated by their forms into groups. The Botrytis group encompasses cauliflowers and broccoli with heads that can range in colour from white and cream to pink, lime green and purple. 'Perfection' is an award-winning mini cauliflower with a cream head that grows to about 10 cm (4 in) in diameter in two months.

Brassica oleracea • *Wild Cabbage*

Description

The cabbage and its relatives are in the Brassicaceae family, which contains only a few species, but many subspecies, groups and cultivars, originates from the temperate coastal areas of Europe and North Africa. Utilized by humans for more than 3,000 years, *Brassicas* serve a multitude of purposes, and are grown for their leaves (cabbages, kale, Asian greens), flowering parts (broccoli, cauliflower, brussels sprouts), seeds (rape/canola), stems (kohlrabi) or roots (turnip, swede).

B. oleracea, also known as Wild Cabbage, is the ancestor of cabbage, broccoli, cauliflower, kale and brussels sprouts, is divided into a number of groups. The Capitata Group is comprised of many forms of cabbage developed in Germany, including the cultivar 'Alba', which is a large cabbage with a flat heavy head and white interior.

Species, variety or cultivar:
Capitata Group, 'Alba'

Other common names:
Wild Cabbage

Height and spread:
40 x 30 cm (16 x 12 in)

Blooming period:
Depends on age of plant and climate

Soil type:
Well-drained moist soil, enriched with well-rotted manure

Sun or Shade:
Needs full sun

Hardiness:
Minimum temp –7°C (20°F)

BELOW: The Wild One (*Brassica oleracea var. oleracea*)

Briza maxima • *Great Quaking Grass*

Description

A species of annual grass that comes from the Mediterranean area and is one of 12 species in the Briza genus, which belongs to the family Poaceae. It has strap-shaped leaves up to 20 cm (8 in) long, and nodding panicles of 7 to 20 heart-shaped flower clusters, light grey or purple, which appear in summer.

The genus name comes from the Greek word *brizo* (to be sleepy or nodding), referring to the delicate panicles of summer-blooming flowers. Briza plants can become invasive in suitable climates, but the flowers are ideal for dried arrangements.

Species, variety or cultivar:
–

Other common names:
Great Quaking Grass

Height and spread:
60 x 20 cm (24 x 8 in)

Blooming period:
Summer

Soil type:
Well-drained cultivated soil, raked fine

Sun or Shade:
Enjoys full sun

Hardiness:
Minimum temp –18°C (0°F)

Calamintha nepeta • *Lesser Calamint*

Description

This spreading rhizome-rooted species is found from Britain to southern Europe, and has downy grey-green stems and leaves, to 3 cm (1¼ in) long. They are strongly aromatic and have small pink to mauve flowers 12 mm (½ in) long, with up to 15 in a cluster, which appear in summer.

Calamint has a long history of medicinal use but these days is usually restricted to just a simple infusion of the leaves, which makes a refreshing tea.

Species, variety or cultivar:
–

Other common names:
Lesser Calamint

Height and spread:
0.8 x 1.5 m (32 x 60 in)

Blooming period:
Summer

Soil type:
Moist, humus-rich, well-drained soil

Sun or Shade:
Likes a bright but not baking position

Hardiness:
Minimum temp –23°C (–10°F)

Calendula officinalis • *Common Marigold*

Description

Originally from southern Europe, but now widely naturalized, this bushy annual has slightly downy, alternate simple leaves and flowers to 8 cm (3 in) in diameter. Successive sowings and dead-heading will result in a display of the cheerful orange or yellow daisies that appear for many months, from spring to summer in cooler areas.

Very easily grown in any well-drained soil in full sun, *C. officinalis* has been used for many centuries for a range of culinary and medicinal purposes.

Species, variety or cultivar:

–

Other common names:

Common Marigold, Pot Marigold, Scotch Marigold

Height and spread:

60 x 45 cm (24 x 18 in)

Blooming period:

Spring to autumn

Soil type:

Any well-drained soil

Sun or Shade:

Prefers full sun

Hardiness:

Minimum temp –23°C (–10°F)

Calendula officinalis • *Common Marigold*

DESCRIPTION

Calendula is a genus of around 20 species of annual and perennial herbs in the daisy (Asteraceae) family. They are found around the Mediterranean area and Atlantic Islands where they are often found growing on disturbed ground, particularly *C. officinalis*, which is a widespread garden escapee. This species, originally from southern Europe, has a number of popular cultivar groups, including the Pacific Beauty Series, which is characterized by tall-stemmed, yellow, orange and apricot flowers that appear for long periods throughout the year.

Species, variety or cultivar:
Pacific Beauty Series

Other common names:
Common Marigold, Pot Marigold, Scotch Marigold

Height and spread:
60 x 45 cm (24 x 18 in)

Blooming period:
Spring to autumn

Soil type:
Any well-drained soil

Sun or Shade:
Prefers full sun

Hardiness:
Minimum temp –23°C (–10°F)

Calibrachoa, hybrid cultivar • *Trailing petunia*

Description

This genus in the nightshade (Solanaceae) family is closely related to *Petunia* and its 25 species are found from southern Brazil across to Peru and Chile, with one species extending north to southern USA. There are a number of hybrid cultivar groups, valued for their low mounding or trailing habit and profusion of small flowers which appear from mid-spring to late autumn or virtually year-round in warm climates.

Flowers in the Colorburst Series come in cherry, red, rose and violet. Apply a weak fertilizer at intervals throughout the growing season, and pinch back the longer shoots to increase the number of flowers.

Species, variety or cultivar:
Colorburst Series, 'Colorburst Violet'

Other common names:
Trailing Petunia

Height and spread:
20 x 60 cm (8 x 24 in)

Blooming period:
Mid-spring to late autumn

Soil type:
A free-draining medium

Sun or Shade:
Thrives in sun or semi-shade

Hardiness:
Minimum temp –12°C (10°F)

Callistephus chinensis • *China Aster*

Species, variety or cultivar:
–
Other common names:
China Aster
Height and spread:
90 x 30 cm (36 x 12 in)
Blooming period:
Summer
Soil type:
Moist, well-drained soil
Sun or Shade:
Likes full sun
Hardiness:
Minimum temp –12°C (10°F)

Description

The sole species in this genus from the daisy (Asteraceae) family is from China. Despite being just one species, it has been developed into an array of varieties, which have flowers in white and all shades of pink, mauve-blue, red and purple. A naturally sturdy upright plant with dark green, pointed oval leaves to over 8 cm (3 in) long, with coarsely toothed edges, *C. chinensis* has flowerheads up to 10 cm (4 in) across, which are borne singly on long stems. Feed occasionally with liquid fertilizer, but err on the cautious side with feeding or you may produce foliage at the expense of flowers.

Calocephalus platycephalus • *Yellow Billy Button*

Description

This is a widespread genus of about 15 species, endemic to Australia, and a member of the daisy (Asteraceae) family. *C. platycephalus* is found in arid and semi-arid areas, and has whitish woolly stems and the leaves are 3 cm (1¼ in) long. The golden yellow flowerheads have no ray florets and are composed of many tiny flowers forming one head. Numerous flowerheads between 12–35 mm (½-1½ in) wide are produced from winter to spring. The genus gets its name from the Greek *kalos* meaning beautiful and *kephalos* meaning head.

Species, variety or cultivar:
–

Other common names:
Yellow Billy Button, Yellow Top

Height and spread:
45 x 45 cm (18 x 18 in)

Blooming period:
Winter to spring

Soil type:
Well-drained soil

Sun or Shade:
Prefers full sun

Hardiness:
Minimum temp –7°C (20°F)

Campanula medium • *Canterbury Bells*

Species, variety or cultivar:
–
Other common names:
Canterbury Bells, Cup and Saucer
Height and spread:
90 x 30 cm (36 x 12 in)
Blooming period:
Summer
Soil type:
Any reasonably fertile well-drained soil
Sun or Shade:
Enjoys full or half sun
Hardiness:
Minimum temp –12°C (10°F)

Description

This large genus has about 300 species and belongs to the bellflower (Campanulaceae) family. C. *medium* is native to southern Europe, with basal rosettes of soft, hairy, lance-shaped leaves. Showy bell-shaped flowers, with recurved rims, on leafy stems, in shades of white, pink or blue, appear in summer. This species is popular for use as cut flowers, and several seed strains are available. Grows easily in any reasonably fertile well-drained soil in sun or half-sun.

Canna, hybrid cultivar • *Canna Lily*

Description

Found throughout the New World in tropical and subtropical areas, and widely naturalized elsewhere, there are just nine species making up the type genus for their family, the Cannaceae. They are vigorous plants with strong, upright, reed-like stems that sprout from rhizomes and which bear long lance-shaped leaves. Heads of lily-like flowers, usually in shades of yellow, tangerine and red, appear throughout the growing season.

There is a large range of garden hybrids with complex and often uncertain parentage, and in a wide range of colours and forms. 'Orange Punch' is a dwarf form growing to 0.9 m (3 ft) and producing stunning flowers of a rich tangerine orange, fading into a yellow throat. Ideal for low beds and borders, they are also suitable for specimen container planting.

The common name Indian Shot comes from the story that the hard black seeds were sometimes substituted for buckshot. They are certainly hard enough for this but are so light that their range would have been extremely limited.

ABOVE: Canna 'Bugle Boy'
In their natural habitat the Canna Lily will attract hummingbirds. Cannas may also fall victim to *canna rust*, a fungus resulting in orange spots on the plant's leaves. Rust infestation is facilitated by overmoist soil.

Species, variety or cultivar:
'Orange Punch'
Other common names:
Canna Lily, Indian Shot
Height and spread:
0.9 x 0.9 m (3 x 3 ft)
Blooming period:
Spring to autumn
Soil type:
Moist, humus-rich, well-drained soil
Sun or Shade:
Likes full sun
Hardiness:
Minimum temp –12°C (10°F)

Canna, hybrid cultivar • *Canna Lily*

Description

This cultivar is one of the taller cultivar in the Canna genus, growing to 2 m (7 ft) tall. 'Tropicanna', also sometimes known as 'Phasion', has bright orange flowers, and its vivid purple-red and yellow-orange striped foliage can make it a striking and contrasting addition to the garden.

Plant in full sun in moist, humus-rich, well-drained soil and feed well. Seeds will often self-sow but rarely result in superior plants. Although from a genus that is often tropical in origin, they can withstand light frosts, as dormant roots, if well insulated with mulch.

Species, variety or cultivar:
'Tropicanna'

Other common names:
Canna Lily, Indian Shot

Height and spread:
2 x 0.9 m (7 x 3 ft)

Blooming period:
Spring to autumn

Soil type:
Moist, humus-rich, well-drained soil

Sun or Shade:
Likes full sun

Hardiness:
Minimum temp –12°C (10°F)

Capsicum annuum • *Bell Pepper*

DESCRIPTION

This genus of ten species, of which five, mainly *C. annuum*, are used by people, belongs to the nightshade (Solonaceae) family. Originating in Mexico and central South America, most capsicums are perennials but are treated as annuals and are grown for their fruit. The Conioides Group of *C. annuum* is comprised of small hot chillies, with erect fruit, more or less conical in shape. 'Thai Miniature', also known as 'Thai Hot Small' is mounded with showy red 2.5 cm (1 in) long fruit.

Species, variety or cultivar:
Conioides Group, 'Thai Miniature'

Other common names:
Bell Pepper, Chilli Pepper, Paprika

Height and spread:
20 x 20 cm (8 x 8 in)

Blooming period:
–

Soil type:
Well-drained, moist soil

Sun or Shade:
Needs full sun

Hardiness:
Minimum temp –23°C (–10°F)

Capsicum annuum • *Bell Pepper*

Description

Annual or short-lived perennials, *C. annuum* has lance-shaped to ovate leaves to 12 cm (5 in) long, and fruits in a range of colours. Although the fruits are traditionally green maturing to red, other colours are becoming common. Cultivar groups are based on the size and shape of the fruit.

The Grossum Group is comprised of sweet bell peppers with bell-shaped or blocky fruit, about 10–12 cm (4–8 in) long, that start off green, and ripen to yellow, orange, red, brown and purple black. 'Mohawk' is a medium sized cultivar, very sweet, and orange when mature.

A well-drained moist soil in full sun is best, with fertilizer applied early in the growing season to bulk up plants. Ease this off as they begin to set fruit. Propagate from seed.

Species, variety or cultivar:
Grossum Group, 'Mohawk'

Other common names:
Bell Pepper, Chilli Pepper, Paprika

Height and spread:
70 x 30 cm (27 x 12 in)

Blooming period:
Spring

Soil type:
Well-drained, moist soil

Sun or Shade:
Needs full sun

Hardiness:
Minimum temp –23°C (–10°F)

ABOVE: The fruit of the *Capsicum annuum* 'Rainbow'
Sweet peppers, or bell peppers, are annuals that have a lovely bushy growing habit. The fruit are green when immature but turn brilliant colours and shapes as they mature. The thick-walled, sweet fruits of 'Rainbow' come in a range of colours, including cream, yellow, orange, red and purple. They look very good served in salads.

Capsicum annuum, ornamental • *Bell Pepper*

DESCRIPTION

Capsicums can be eaten fresh, pickled, smoked, dried, tinned or roasted. There are two main types of capsicums – hot or chilli peppers, hot to taste, and sweet or bell peppers, which are not so hot. Some types however, are grown purely for ornamental purposes, even though they are usually edible. These comprise the Ornamental Forms, which have fruits that are held upright, in a range of colours, and which are good short-term houseplants or for the greenhouse. 'Nosegay Pepper' is 15–20 cm (6–8 in) tall, and is a colourful mix of tiny fruits in red, orange and green.

Species, variety or cultivar:
'Nosegay Pepper'

Other common names:
Bell Pepper, Chilli Pepper, Paprika

Height and spread:
20 x 20 cm (8 x 8 in)

Blooming period:
–

Soil type:
Well-drained, moist soil

Sun or Shade:
Needs full sun

Hardiness:
Minimum temp –23°C (–10°F)

Catharanthus roseus • *Madagascar Periwinkle*

DESCRIPTION

All eight species of this genus are from Madagascar, and although related to the common periwinkle (*Vinca*), are less hardy and tolerate little or no frost. *C. Roseus* is an upright species, having glossy deep green leaves with a pale midrib, to 5 cm (2 in) long. 'Blue Pearl' has white-centred lavender-blue to mauve coloured, 5-petalled flowers, with a yellow 'eye'. They are very easily grown in sun or part-shade, and are drought tolerant but flower more heavily with summer moisture. Pinch back to encourage bushiness, and in cool areas where winter frost would be fatal, bring indoors or discard and replace in spring.

Species, variety or cultivar:
'Blue Pearl'

Other common names:
Madagascar Periwinkle, Periwinkle, Rosy Periwinkle

Height and spread:
45 x 40 cm (18 x 16 in)

Blooming period:
Spring to summer

Soil type:
Moderately fertile, well-drained soil

Sun or Shade:
Easily grown in sun or part-shade

Hardiness:
Minimum temp 4°C (40°F)

Catharanthus roseus • *Madagascar Periwinkle*

Species, variety or cultivar:
Pacifica Series, 'Pacifica Red'

Other common names:
Madagascar Periwinkle, Periwinkle, Rosy Periwinkle

Height and spread:
45 x 40 cm (18 x 16 in)

Blooming period:
Summer

Soil type:
Moderately fertile, well-drained soil

Sun or Shade:
Easily grown in sun or part-shade

Hardiness:
Minimum temp 4°C (40°F)

Description

Although considered a weed in the tropics and subtropics, the commonly cultivated species C. *roseus* is often grown as a greenhouse plant or summer bedder in temperate gardens. Naturally highly toxic, it is the source of vinca alkaloids, used to treat lymphocytic leukaemia and Hodgkin's Disease. The species is divided into a number of subgroups, such as the Pacifica Series, and 'Pacifica Red', a member of this series, has attractive dark pink-red 5-petalled flowers that appear in summer.

Celosia argentea • *Cockscomb*

DESCRIPTION

This genus is found in the tropics of Asia, Africa, and the Americas, has about 50 species of annuals and perennials, and belongs to the amaranth (Amaranthaceae) family. *C. argentea* var. *cristata*, an annual, is the only widely cultivated species. Upright plants, some are up to 1.8 m (6 ft) tall, though most are far smaller. They have simple lance-shaped leaves up to 15 cm (6 in) long and tiny vivid yellow, orange or red flowers massed in upright plumes or combs.

The name *Celosia* comes from a Greek word, *Kelos*, meaning burning, which is a very appropriate reference to the flame-like colours and shape of the flowerhead.

Species, variety or cultivar:
var. cristata

Other common names:
Cockscomb, Woolflower

Height and spread:
1.8 x 0.6 m (6 x 2 ft)

Blooming period:
Summer

Soil type:
Fertile, well-drained soil

Sun or Shade:
Prefers full sun

Hardiness:
Minimum temp 4°C (40°F)

Celosia argentea • *Cockscomb*

DESCRIPTION

This species has been developed into many forms available with green, purple or red foliage and many flower colours and styles. The Plumosa Group has upright plumes of flowers, not always terminal, and within this group 'Forest Fire' has vivid red plumes and red foliage.

Although as an annual it can be grown far outside its natural tropical range, *Celosia* needs ample warmth to perform well. Plant in fertile well-drained soil in full sun and water well. Raise from seed.

Species, variety or cultivar:
var. cristata, Plumosa Group, 'Forest Fire'

Other common names:
Cockscomb, Woolflower

Height and spread:
0.6 x 0.6 m (2 x 2 ft)

Blooming period:
Summer

Soil type:
Fertile, well-drained soil

Sun or Shade:
Prefers full sun

Hardiness:
Minimum temp 4°C (40°F)

Centaurea cyanus • *Bachelor's Button*

Description

An annual or biennial from temperate Eurasia, this species has narrow green to blue-green leaves, sometimes silvery when young. The thistle-like flowerheads, which emerge from an egg-shaped receptacle known as an involucre, are usually blue in species, but garden forms include white and a wide range of pink and blue shades.

Plant in full sun and light, in well-drained soil. Good ventilation will remove any mildew problems, and dead-heading will prolong flowering. The genus is named after the Greek mythological centaur, half-horse, half-man, famed for his healing powers, as some species were used traditionally to treat wounds.

Species, variety or cultivar:
–

Other common names:
Bachelor's Button, Bluebottle, Cornflower

Height and spread:
90 x 40 cm (36 x 16 in)

Blooming period:
Summer

Soil type:
Light, well-drained soil

Sun or Shade:
Enjoys full sun

Hardiness:
Minimum temp –46°C (–50°F)

Chenopodium giganteum • *Tree Spinach*

Description

One of the most familiar genera in the goosefoot (Chenopodiaceae) family, *Chenopodium* consists of about 100 species of annuals and evergreen or deciduous perennials and shrubs, and is found in temperate climates around the world including arid regions and saline areas. Some of the annuals are widespread weeds, others are grown as garden flowers, leaf vegetable, herbs or grain crops or valued as fodder plants.

C. giganteum is an annual species from northern India, with leaves up to 15 cm (6 in) long. The much-branched growing shoots are purple-tipped, and the elongated summer–autumn flower clusters are also purple. Flowers are tiny and crowded in clusters in the leaf axils or on terminal panicles; grain like fruits are hardly larger but profuse, developing within the persistent perianth. Grown as a bedding annual for foliage colour, the leaves are edible. Easily grown in any garden soil in full sun, they are tough drought-tolerant plants.

LEFT AND BELOW: An attractive and valuable plant for borders with purple and lush green foliage. Good as a pot plant or centrepiece. Chenopodium can be sown outdoors where they flower during May once the soil has warmed. Keep moist until after germination and thin out to 30 cm (12 in) apart.

Species, variety or cultivar:
–
Other common names:
Tree Spinach
Height and spread:
3 x 0.9 m (10 x 3 ft)
Blooming period:
Summer to autumn
Soil type:
Any garden soil
Sun or Shade:
Likes full sun
Hardiness:
Minimum temp –12°C (10°F)

Clarkia amoena • *Satin Flower*

Species, variety or cultivar:
–
Other common names:
Satin Flower
Height and spread:
60 x 30 cm (24 x 12 in)
Blooming period:
Late spring to summer
Soil type:
Moderately fertile well-drained soil
Sun or Shade:
Enjoys full sun
Hardiness:
Minimum temp –18°C (0°F)

Description

This genus of 33 species of annual herbs belongs to the evening primrose (Onagraceae) family. The majority are native to North America, where they grow in dry open areas in forests, such as *C. amoena*, which is a showy species from northern California. It bears densely packed spikes of cup-shaped flowers of pink to lavender, sometimes darkening at the base or shading to white, and with centres usually splashed with dark red.

All *Clarkia* species dislike hot humid conditions, so in warmer areas seed should be sown in autumn so that the plants will flower before the summer heat becomes intense. In cooler areas sow in early spring.

Cleome sesquiorygalis • *Spider Flower*

Description

An upright annual from southern Brazil, Paraguay, and northern Argentina, this species has palmate leaves with five to seven finely toothed hairy leaflets to over 10 cm (4 in) long. The 4-petalled flowers have long, filament-like stamens and are carried in apical heads with the filaments facing outwards, hence the name spider flower. They are clustered in terminal heads, and the petals are 3 cm (1¼ in) long. There are several seedling strains and named forms, such as the Queen Series, with varieties such as 'Pink Queen', named after their flower colour. In the USA Cleome has long been associated with US President Thomas Jefferson's famous garden at Monticello.

Species, variety or cultivar:
'Pink Queen'

Other common names:
Spider Flower

Height and spread:
1.5 x 0.5 m (60 x 20 in)

Blooming period:
Summer

Soil type:
Moist, fertile, free-draining soil

Sun or Shade:
Likes a sheltered sunny position

Hardiness:
Minimum temp –1°C (30°F)

Coix lacryma-jobi • *Christ's Tears*

Species, variety or cultivar:
–
Other common names:
Christ's Tears, Job's Tears
Height and spread:
120 x 100 cm (48 x 40 in)
Blooming period:
–
Soil type:
Moist to damp soil
Sun or Shade:
Prefers a sunny sheltered spot
Hardiness:
Minimum temp –7°C (20°F)

Description

Coix is a small genus of six species of annual and perennial plants in the grass (Poaceae) family that come from tropical Asia, and are now naturalized in many other parts of the world. *C. lacryma-jobi* is the only species of ornamental value, and has lush bright green arching leaves, to 50 cm (20 in) long, and hard jet-black seeds to 12 mm (0.5 in) in diameter, that have been used as rosary beads.

Grow in moist to damp soil in a sheltered sunny spot and plant after frosts have finished in areas where these occur. Ideal for aquatic/wet gardens.

Colocasia esculenta • *Cocoyam*

DESCRIPTION

Native to tropical eastern Asia, this species is widely grown throughout tropical regions as a food crop, and has prominently veined dark green leaves to 60 cm (24 in) long, which are arrow- or heart-shaped, with sturdy stems supporting them from below. In tropical areas the roots of C. *esculenta* are a staple food, and are cooked in a variety of ways. Elsewhere they are grown for the ornamental quality of their leaves.

Cultivars are also grown ornamentally, such as 'Fontanesii', which has dark purple stems, and dark green leaves with purple veins. In suitably warm climates grow in a fertile moisture-retentive soil, watering well in dry spells.

Species, variety or cultivar:
'Fontanesii'

Other common names:
Cocoyam, Taro

Height and spread:
1.8 x 1.8 m (6 x 6 ft)

Blooming period:
–

Soil type:
Fertile, moisture-retentive soil

Sun or Shade:
Needs full sun

Hardiness:
Minimum temp –7°C (20°F)

Consolida ajacis • *Larkspur*

Description

This species is a Mediterranean native with lacy finely cut foliage in basal clumps and with wiry upright stems carrying heads of many spurred flowers in shades of blue, pink or white. Garden forms occur in a wide colour range and include double flowers.

The Giant Imperial Series has double flowers covering the entire colour range with long spikes that last well and keep their colour when dried. Members of this group, such as 'Giant Imperial Pink Perfection', are named for their colour. Raise from seed, and plant in full sun in a fertile well-drained soil. They may need staking.

Species, variety or cultivar:
'Giant Imperial Pink Perfection'

Other common names:
Larkspur

Height and spread:
100 x 30 cm (40 x 12 in)

Blooming period:
Summer

Soil type:
Fertile, well-drained soil

Sun or Shade:
Enjoys full sun

Hardiness:
Minimum temp –7°C (20°F)

Convolvulus tricolor • *Dwarf Morning Glory*

DESCRIPTION

This species is found through southern Europe and North Africa, and has small, pointed, oval leaves and flowers up to 5 cm (2 in) wide, borne singly in the leaf axils, in blue shades, often with a yellow throat. The widely flared funnel-shaped flowers bloom in succession over a long period. Hardy plants, they are adaptable to a range of soils and situations, but prefer a sunny position. They are easily propagated from cuttings.

Species, variety or cultivar:
–

Other common names:
Dwarf Morning Glory

Height and spread:
100 x 80 cm (40 x 32 in)

Blooming period:
Summer

Soil type:
Hardy plants, these are adaptable to a wide range of soils

Sun or Shade:
Prefer a position in full sun

Hardiness:
Minimum temp –12°C (10°F)

Coreopsis tinctoria • *Tickseed*

DESCRIPTION

This genus, found in the Americas, especially in southwestern USA and Mexico, has 80-odd annuals and perennials, and is a member of the daisy (Asteraceae) family. They are compact plants that flower profusely, providing spectacular summer colour, nearly always golden yellow, though garden forms occur in many shades.

C. tinctoria is a summer-flowering annual found over much of North America, and has leaves that are usually narrow and entire, sometimes pinnate, to 10 cm (4 in) long. The species has many small flowerheads, with yellow ray florets, reddening at the base, and disc florets of red-brown. Both the common name tickseed and the Greek word *coreopsis* (bug-like), from which the proper name is derived, refer to the appearance of the small black seeds.

Plant in a sunny position in light well-drained soil. Although they flower better with summer moisture, they are quite drought tolerant.

LEFT AND ABOVE: These flowers are also great for cutting. It is called 'calliopsis' in the South, where it is enjoyed right down into Florida. In fact, the *coreopsis* was recently designated as the official State Wildflower of Florida.

Species, variety or cultivar:
–

Other common names:
Tickseed

Height and spread:
1.2 x 0.6 m (48 x 24 in)

Blooming period:
Summer

Soil type:
Light, well-drained soil

Sun or Shade:
Full or half sun

Hardiness:
Minimum temp –7°C (20°F)

Cosmos bipinnatus • *Mexican Aster*

Description

This genus of the daisy (Asteraceae) family is found in the Americas from the tropics to the warm temperate zones. It comprises 26 species, including both annuals and perennials, of which three are commonly grown. The common annual cosmos, *C. bipinnatus*, is an annual native to Mexico and southern USA, with ferny pinnate leaves to over 10 cm (4 in) long, and very fine narrow leaflets. The showy, large, wide-open flowers are long-stemmed, and have eight ray florets, pink to lavender in the wild, but with many garden forms and seedling strains. The species is available in many colours and varieties, from dwarf to 1.8 m (6 ft) tall.

The Sonata Series has tall, simple, daisy-like flowers in pink and white shades, either single colours such as 'Sonata Pink', or mixed. Plant out when all danger of frost has passed, in full sun with moist, well-drained soil. Do not overfeed or the plants may become top-heavy; they may need staking anyway.

Species, variety or cultivar:
Sonata Series, 'Sonata Pink'

Other common names:
Mexican Aster

Height and spread:
90 x 90 cm (3 x 3 ft)

Blooming period:
Summer

Soil type:
Moist, well-drained soil

Sun or Shade:
Likes half to full sun

Hardiness:
Minimum temp –18°C (0°F)

LEFT AND ABOVE: Cosmos is easy to germinate, has spectacular flowers that are great for cutting, and is virtually pest free – these attributes make it great for kids and beginners. Cosmos flowers are also perfect for pressing.

Cosmos sulphureus • *Mexican Aster*

Description

This annual species is found from northern South America to Mexico, and has pinnate, sometimes faintly hairy leaves to 35 cm (14 in) long. The summer-borne flowerheads range from yellow through orange to red, and there are several seedling strains.

'Cosmic Yellow' has attractive bright yellow single and semi-double flowers to 60 cm (24 in) tall, and is ideal as a colour feature or as a ground cover. Native Americans treated the young tops of *C. sulphureus* as a vegetable.

Species, variety or cultivar:
'Cosmic Yellow'

Other common names:
Mexican Aster

Height and spread:
60 x 60 cm (24 x 24 in)

Blooming period:
Summer

Soil type:
Moist, well-drained soil

Sun or Shade:
Likes half to full sun

Hardiness:
Minimum temp –18°C (0°F)

Cucumis melo • *Honeydew*

Description

This is a species of annual vines found in arid regions of Africa, Arabia, southwest Asia and Australia. Wild types may be bitter, but cultivars produce a range of generally round sweet fruit with either smooth or rough skins.

The Reticulatus Group is comprised of netted melons, in assorted shapes and sizes. Skins can be ribbed, warty or smooth, as well as netted. The seed cavity is large in old varieties, smaller in new varieties. Some varieties (muskmelons) have a musky aroma. 'Ambrosia' has firm, luscious, extra sweet, juicy, peach-coloured flesh, and a fragrant aroma when ripe.

Species, variety or cultivar:
–

Other common names:
Cantaloupe, Honeydew melon, Muskmelon

Height and spread:
0.7 x 3 m (28 x 120 in)

Blooming period:
–

Soil type:
Moist, humus-rich soil

Sun or Shade:
Needs full sun

Hardiness:
Minimum temp –7°C (20°F)

Cucumis sativus • *Cucumber*

Description

There are a great number of different forms in this species, including field, greenhouse, gherkin, Sikkim, apple and snake cucumbers. Some are more tolerant of cold or more 'burpless' than others. Some varieties need a frame to climb on; others do not.

'Spacemaster' is disease resistant, compact and slender, with dark green fruit, good for pickling when small and for slicing when mature. Grow from seed, ideally in a rich soil with lots of organic matter and a constant supply of moisture during the long warm growing period. In regions where summers are short they are often grown in greenhouses.

Species, variety or cultivar:
'Spacemaster'
Other common names:
Cucumber, Gherkin
Height and spread:
0.5 x 3 m (20 x 120 in)
Blooming period:
–
Soil type:
Rich soil with lots of organic matter and a constant supply of moisture
Sun or Shade:
Prefers full sun
Hardiness:
Minimum temp –7°C (20°F)

Cucurbita pepo • *Courgette*

Description

A trailing or climbing genus of about 27 species of annuals and perennials from North and South America, in the pumpkin (Cucurbitaceae) family, grown for both their edible and their ornamental fruit. *C. pepo* is a trailing or bushy species that has many cultivars. The leaves are lobed, triangular and prickly, and the young leaves and flowers can also be eaten. Most varieties are best eaten straight after harvest.

'Black Beauty' has long, straight, smooth, dark green fruit, best eaten when 15–20 cm (6–8 in) long. A rich well-drained soil in full sun and a long warm growing season are essential for producing a good crop.

Species, variety or cultivar:
'Black Beauty'
Other common names:
Courgette, Summer Squash, Vegetable Marrow, Zucchini
Height and spread:
0.5 x 3 m (20 x 120 in)
Blooming period:
–
Soil type:
Very rich well-drained soil
Sun or Shade:
Prefers full sun
Hardiness:
Minimum temp –12°C (10°F)

Cuphea x purpurea • *Celosia*

Description

This bushy subshrub is a garden hybrid between *C. Ilavea* and *C. procumbens*. They have dark green, lance-shaped, pointed leaves and narrow, tubular, deep pink to purplish flowers which appear from late spring through autumn.

Fairly frost tender, this species does best in full sun or light shade, in well-drained moist soil, with protection from strong winds. Occasional tip pruning from an early age will encourage compact growth. Propagation is from seed or from tip cuttings.

Species, variety or cultivar:
–

Other common names:
Celosia

Height and spread:
75 x 75 cm (30 x 30 in)

Blooming period:
Late spring to autumn

Soil type:
Well-drained moist soil

Sun or Shade:
Do best in full sun or light shade

Hardiness:
Minimum temp –7°C (20°F)

Cynara cardunculus • *Cardoon*

DESCRIPTION

There are ten species of herbs in this genus, which belongs to the daisy (Asteraceae) family. They are native to the Mediterranean, northwestern Africa and the Canary Islands. The plants resemble giant thistles, having large leaves with pointed lobes, sometimes spiny, and tall heads of thistle-like flowers.

C. cardunculatus is from Mediterranean regions, is a statuesque plant which has thick, pointed-lobed, greyish leaves to 1.5 m (5 ft) long. Large, purple, thistle-like flowers stand above the foliage in summer. Although mainly grown ornamentally, the young stems can be cooked as a vegetable. Grow in full sun in a well-drained soil, sheltered from strong winds, and allow plenty of space for the large heavy leaves to develop.

Species, variety or cultivar:
–
Other common names:
Cardoon
Height and spread:
2.4 x 2.4 m (8 x 8 ft)
Blooming period:
Summer
Soil type:
Well-drained soil
Sun or Shade:
Enjoys full sun
Hardiness:
Minimum temp –23°C (–10°F)

Dahlia • *Dahlia*

Description

Although breeders are currently trying to introduce other species into the mix, virtually all of our modern garden dahlias are *D. coccinea x D. pinnata* hybrids, a cross that first appeared in Madrid, Spain, in 1789, not long after dahlias arrived in Europe from Mexico.

The many hybrid cultivars are divided into different groups, such as the Decorative Group, which is characterized by a double style, with no central disc, and broad, flat or slightly involute florets making a rounded head. In some classifications this group is subdivided into formal (very even petals that are neatly arranged) and informal (more open and less regular). The flowers are classified as giant, large, medium, small or miniature depending on their size. Giant flowers do not, however, necessarily mean giant plants: some of the largest flowers are borne on relatively small plants. 'Arabian Night' is a deep black-red cultivar, turning red, and lightening with age.

LEFT AND BELOW: The dahlia is the national flower of Mexico. In 1872 a box of dahlia roots were sent from Mexico to Holland. The impact of this long journey was devastating in that all but one tuber failed to make the crossing. This singular root, however, proved quite astonishing in that it produced a brilliant red bloom with petals that were rolled back and pointed. Immediately dahlias regained their place on the benches of plant breeders who began to successfully combine this new variety (*D. juarezii*) with parents of early varieties and their progenies have served as the parents of today's hybrids.

Species, variety or cultivar:
Group 5: Decorative, 'Arabian Night'

Other common names:
–

Height and spread:
90 x 90 cm (3 x 3 ft)

Blooming period:
Summer

Soil type:
Moist, fertile, humus-rich, well-drained soil

Sun or Shade:
Either full sun or partial shade

Hardiness:
Minimum temp –7°C (20°F)

Dahlia • *Dahlia*

Species, variety or cultivar:
Group 6: Ball, 'Charles Dickens'
Other common names:
–
Height and spread:
90 x 90 cm (3 x 3 ft)
Blooming period:
Summer
Soil type:
Moist, fertile, humus-rich, well-drained soil
Sun or Shade:
Either full sun or partial shade
Hardiness:
Minimum temp –7°C (20°F)

Description

The ball group of dahlia cultivars is characterized by ball-shaped flowers that are globular, but which may be slightly flattened on top. The ray florets are broad, rounded at the tips, and involute for half their length. They are divided by flower size into miniature, up to 10 cm (4 in) in diameter; small, 10–15 cm (4–6 in) in diameter; medium, 15–20 cm (6–8 in) in diameter; and large, over 20 cm (8 in) across.

'Charles Dickens' is a popular ball cultivar of small pink flowers. They do best in full sun or partial shade, with moist, fertile, humus-rich, well-drained soil. Do not crowd, as good air circulation lessens the risk of mildew.

Dahlia • *Dahlia*

Description

The Pompon Group of dahlias has flowerheads that are nearly spherical, and is similar to the ball style, but with smaller flowers that give the impression of more tightly packed florets. Florets are involute for their entire length. 'Lollipop' has pinkish to mauve outer ray florets, which age to pale pink.

Dahlias prefer full sun or partial shade, with moist, fertile, humus-rich, well-drained soil. Tubers cannot be left in the ground over winter in areas where the soil freezes, or where they will become waterlogged. In such locations, lift the tubers, and store them in dry sand or sawdust in a frost-free place.

Species, variety or cultivar:
Group 7: Pompon, 'Lollipop'

Other common names:
–

Height and spread:
90 x 90 cm (3 x 3 ft)

Blooming period:
Summer

Soil type:
Moist, fertile, humus-rich, well-drained soil

Sun or Shade:
Either full sun or partial shade

Hardiness:
Minimum temp –7°C (20°F)

Dahlia • *Decorative Dahlia*

Description

Named after the Swedish botanist Dr Andreas Dahl (1751–89), the genus *Dahlia* has around 30 tuberous-rooted species in the daisy (Asteraceae) family, originating from Mexico and as far south as Colombia. Almost all forms are immediately recognizable, with similar pinnate foliage, hollow cane-like stems, and bright flowerheads.

The Cactus Group of dahlia cultivars has fully double flowers with long quilled ray florets and no central disc. The quilling extends for at least half the length of the floret. Both cactus and semi-cactus forms are further subdivided into large- and small-flowered types and are available in a range of colours. 'Orange Marmalade' is an attractive orange cultivar, as the name suggests.

Most dahlias reach their peak of bloom after the longest day and continue to flower until frost or winter cold intervenes. Tops die with first frosts, but provided the soil does not freeze or become waterlogged, tubers can be left in the ground for winter.

Species, variety or cultivar:
Group 8: Cactus, 'Orange Marmalade'

Other common names:
Decorative Dahlia

Height and spread:
90 x 90 cm (3 x 3 ft)

Blooming period:
Summer

Soil type:
Moist, fertile, humus-rich, well-drained soil

Sun or Shade:
Either full sun or partial shade

Hardiness:
Minimum temp –7°C (20°F)

LEFT AND ABOVE RIGHT: The Cactus Group of dahlias make a good display in a mixed border from mid-summer right until the first winter frost strikes and are excellent for the vase.

Dahlia • *Dahlia*

Description

The Semi-cactus Group of dahlia hybrids are not semi-double-flowered cactus forms, but fully double flowers with broad-based ray florets that are quilled for less than half their length. They may be straight or incurving. 'Royal Wedding' is an appealing orange and yellow example of the group.

As with all other groups, members of the Semi-cactus Group of dahlias prefer full sun or partial shade, with moist, fertile, humus-rich, well-drained soil. And, as with all dahlias, if the soil is likely to freeze, or become waterlogged, the tubers should be removed from and stored elsewhere, in dry sand or sawdust, for the winter.

Species, variety or cultivar:
Group 9: Semi-cactus, 'Royal Wedding'

Other common names:
–

Height and spread:
90 x 90 cm (3 x 3 ft)

Blooming period:
Summer

Soil type:
Moist, fertile, humus-rich, well-drained soil

Sun or Shade:
Either full sun or partial shade

Hardiness:
Minimum temp –7°C (20°F)

Dahlia imperialis • *Tree Dahlia*

Species, variety or cultivar:
–
Other common names:
Tree Dahlia
Height and spread:
8 x 4.5 m (25 x 15 ft)
Blooming period:
Autumn
Soil type:
Moist, fertile, humus-rich, well-drained soil
Sun or Shade:
Either full sun or partial shade
Hardiness:
Minimum temp –7°C (20°F)

Description

Although dahlias are almost always immediately recognizable by their foliage, stems and flowerheads, there is a large variation in forms. Wild species usually have single blooms but the many fancy-flowered garden form range in styles and colours. There is also a large variation between the species themselves, from dwarf through to tree-sized species that can grow to over 6 m (20 ft) high in one season.

Such a tree-sized species is *D. imperialis*, which is found from Guatemala to Colombia, and has huge bamboo-like stems, and many-flowered clusters of pink to lavender flowerheads. The species blooms late, and is often cut by frost before flowering in temperate climates.

Datura stramonium • *Common Thorn Apple*

Description

This genus of 11 species from southern North America is now widely naturalized in much of the world, and belongs to the nightshade (Solonaceae) family. They are annuals with dry capsular fruit and erect flowers, compared with Brugmansia (the 'daturas' of tropical horticulture), which have fleshy fruit and drooping flowers.

D. stramonium has coarsely toothed leaves, which have an unpleasant odour when crushed, and spiny fruits. Short-lived tubular flowers, arising from leaf axils, or forks in the branches, are white or purple and appear in summer. The plant contains powerful alkaloids, which can be highly toxic, though they have been used as hallucinogens by Native Americans.

Species, variety or cultivar:
Stramonium

Other common names:
Common Thorn Apple, Jamestown Weed, Jimson's Weed

Height and spread:
1.8 x 1.8 m (6 x 6 ft)

Blooming period:
Summer

Soil type:
Well-drained soil

Sun or Shade:
Full sun

Hardiness:
Minimum temp –18°C (0°F)

Delphinium • *Larkspur*

Species, variety or cultivar:
Hybrid cultivar, 'Blue Lagoon'

Other common names:
Larkspur, Annual Delphinium

Height and spread:
2 x 0.9 m (7 x 3 ft)

Blooming period:
Spring to summer

Soil type:
Moist, humus-rich, fertile soil

Sun or Shade:
Prefers full sun

Hardiness:
Minimum temp –40°C (–40°F)

Description

A member of the buttercup (Ranunculaceae) family, Delphinium consists of around 250 species of annuals, biennials and perennials. Plant sizes vary markedly with the species: the smaller species may not exceed 30 cm (12 in) tall, while the fancy hybrids can grow to over 2 m (7 ft). Flower colours vary, but the genus is best known for the intense blue flowers it often produces. 'Blue Lagoon' is a medium to tall cultivar, its flowers being a pure blue, with a light eye.

An open airy position is best, as this lessens the risk of mildew, however, the more exposed the position, the more important it is that the plants are staked to prevent damage from the wind.

Dianthus barbatus • *Sweet William*

DESCRIPTION

From the Eurasian region, this genus is commonly known as carnations or pinks. Most species have narrow, somewhat grassy, blue-green leaves emerging directly from a dense basal clump or on wiry spreading stems. The foliage colour is a perfect foil for the flowers, which in the species are simple 5-petalled structures often powerfully fragrant, with a spicy scent. Flower stem length varies greatly, and although the flower colour is generally pink, the common name, pinks, refers to the ragged petal edges, which appear as if cut with pinking shears.

D. barbatus, a short-lived, southern European perennial is one of 300 or so species in the genus, and is usually grown as an annual. It comprises a clump of lance-shaped leaves, with pinked flowers clustered in heads. Seedling strains are available in many colours and patterned forms, such as the Auricula-eyed Mixed Group, which has a contrasting coloured ring near the centre.

LEFT AND ABOVE: This close relative of the carnation is one of the wildflowers that was taken directly into gardens from the wild. Of course, there are also hundreds of hybrids made from this flower and others in the 'pink' family. The wide range of colours and bi-coloured blooms make this a truly spectacular wildflower in meadows.

Species, variety or cultivar:
Auricula-eyed Mixed Group

Other common names:
Sweet William, Carnation

Height and spread:
60 x 30 cm (24 x 12 in)

Blooming period:
Spring

Soil type:
Moist, well-drained, humus-rich soil

Sun or Shade:
Likes a bright position

Hardiness:
Minimum temp –34°C (–30°F)

Dianthus • *Carnation*

DESCRIPTION

Although sometimes really perennial, these small plants are grown as annuals. In many ways they resemble Sweet William (*D. barbatus*), but they are available in a wider range of sizes and growth forms, including some available for hanging baskets. The Floral Lace Series is a popular subgroup, with masses of small flowers with pinked edges. 'Floral Lace Crimson' is a deep crimson-red, with lighter pink borders.

As with all Dianthus forms, plant in a bright, open position in moist, well-drained, humus-rich soil. They appreciate a little lime and need regular feeding to prevent the centre of the clump from dying out. Propagate from seed or small basal cuttings known as 'slips', or by division.

Species, variety or cultivar:
Annual Bedding, 'Floral Lace Crimson'

Other common names:
Carnation

Height and spread:
60 x 30 cm (24 x 12 in)

Blooming period:
Spring

Soil type:
Moist, well-drained, humus-rich soil

Sun or Shade:
Likes a bright position

Hardiness:
Minimum temp –34°C (–30°F)

Echium plantagineum • *Paterson's Curse*

Description

A hairy-leafed annual or biennial from Europe, this species is often weedy elsewhere, especially in Australia, where it is known as Paterson's Curse and stretches for miles across plains. The pinkish red buds are borne in spikes, opening to intense reddish or violet blue tubular flowers, to 3 cm (1¼ in) long, in late spring–summer. 'Blue Bedder' (syn. *E. vulgare* 'Blue Bedder'), is a shorter form of purple blooms.

Thriving with only moderate amounts of fertilizer and water, they do best in full sun. Position them carefully in milder climates, due to their tendency to self-sow.

Species, variety or cultivar:
'Blue Bedder'

Other common names:
Paterson's Curse, Purple Viper's Bugloss

Height and spread:
90 x 45 cm (36 x 18 in)

Blooming period:
Late spring through summer

Soil type:
Thrives with only moderate amounts of fertilizer and water

Sun or Shade:
Does best in full sun

Hardiness:
Minimum temp –12°C (10°F)

Emilia sonchifolia • *Flora's Paintbrush*

Description

There are about 24 species of rather sparse annual herbs in this genus, belonging to the daisy (Asteraceae) family. They are found throughout Polynesia, India and tropical Africa. Their foliage is reminiscent of sow thistles, and the finely rayed flowers are borne singly or in small corymbs.

E. sonchifolia is from tropical Asia and Africa, and is an annual that produces rosettes of lyre-shaped leaves, sometimes bluish green. The tassel-like flowers bloom in shades of scarlet, brilliant orange or yellow in summer. They are easily grown in most soils in full sun, and should be planted close together for the best effect.

Species, variety or cultivar:
–

Other common names:
Flora's Paintbrush, Tassel Flower

Height and spread:
50 x 25 cm (20 x 10 in)

Blooming period:
Summer

Soil type:
Easily grown in most soils

Sun or Shade:
Best in full sun

Hardiness:
Minimum temp –7°C (20°F)

Eschscholzia californica • *California poppy*

Species, variety or cultivar:
–
Other common names:
California poppy
Height and spread:
60 x 40 cm (24 x 16 in)
Blooming period:
Summer
Soil type:
Light, gritty, well-drained soil
Sun or Shade:
Enjoys a sunny position
Hardiness:
Minimum temp –23°C (–10°F)

Description

From western USA and northern Baja California, Mexico, this species has naturalized elsewhere, and is now a weed in much of Australia. It is an annual or short-lived perennial, with leaves that are variable but usually finely divided, feathery and blue-green. The flowers grow to over 5 cm (2 in) across, are usually orange but often yellow, rarely cream or pink.

Very easily grown in any sunny position with light, gritty, well-drained soil, it often self-sows and naturalizes, especially in gravel riverbeds. Propagate from seed, which is best sown directly where it is required to grow.

Eschscholzia cultivar • *California poppy*

Description

Native to western North America, and now widely naturalized, this genus in the poppy (Papaveraceae) family is made up of about eight annuals and short-lived perennials. It was named in 1820 for Johann Friedrich Eschscholtz (1793–1831), the leader of the Russian expedition on which it was first collected, in 1816. (The 't' in his name was somehow lost in the transcription.) The seeds were among the many David Douglas took to England.

California poppies have fine, feathery foliage, often a rather greyish green, and in summer produce masses of bright golden yellow 4- to 8-petalled poppies that only open on sunny days. Modern seed strains come in many flower colours, and the flowers are followed by long seed capsules. Most are very frost hardy and will tolerate poor soil, provided it is well-drained. Propagate from seed, which is best sown in spring directly where the plant will grow, as they do not like transplanting.

Species, variety or cultivar:
–
Other common names:
California poppy
Height and spread:
60 x 40 cm (24 x 16 in)
Blooming period:
Summer
Soil type:
Light, gritty, well-drained soil
Sun or Shade:
Enjoys a sunny position
Hardiness:
Minimum temp –23°C (–10°F)

LEFT AND ABOVE RIGHT: As undemanding annuals, these plants are ideal for filling large areas of ground with colour. They require little care and reward with colourful blooms.

Eschscholzia lobii • *Frying Pans*

Description

Native to California's Central Valley, USA, and is common on the Sierra Nevada side. This annual has sticky green foliage and stems, with grass-like leaves that are finely divided and clumped at the base. The bright yellow flowers, to 5 cm (2 in) across, which sit atop long naked stems, appear in summer. This species is similar to *E. caespitosa*, and is often sold under that name.

Like *E. californica, E. lobbii* is very easily grown in any sunny position with light, gritty, well-drained soil, and often self-sows and naturalizes. Propagation is from seed, best sown directly where it is required to grow.

Species, variety or cultivar:
–

Other common names:
Frying Pans

Height and spread:
30 x 30 cm (12 x 12 in)

Blooming period:
Summer

Soil type:
Light, gritty, well-drained soil

Sun or Shade:
Likes full sun

Hardiness:
Minimum temp –18°C (0°F)

Euphorbia marginata • *Ghost Weed*

Description

This annual, native to North America, is usually cultivated in gardens in low-growing forms. It produces a dense mound of light green, soft, downy leaves, to 8 cm (3 in) long, edged in white, sometimes entirely white, at the top of the plant. White bracts of flowers appear in summer. Care should be taken to avoid the milky sap, which can cause severe dermatological problems.

The showy leaves of this species make a good contrast in the garden to brightly coloured flowers. Relatively quick-growing, the plant prefers full sun, but can cope with half sun. It will survive cold conditions, and is well suited to rockery gardens.

Species, variety or cultivar:
–

Other common names:
Ghost Weed, Snow On The Mountain

Height and spread:
100 x 50 cm (40 x 20 in)

Blooming period:
Summer

Soil type:
Well-drained soil, damp but not wet

Sun or Shade:
Full or half sun

Hardiness:
Minimum temp –34°C (–30°F)

Euryale ferox • *Prickly water lily*

Description

This genus, comprising just one species found from northern India to China and Japan, belongs to the waterlily (Nymphaeaceae) family. The leaves, which are round, have a dull green, puckered upper surface, and a reddish, strongly ribbed and very prickly, lower surface, and are up to 1.5 m (5 ft) across. The red to purple or lilac summer-borne flowers often do not open, remaining more or less submerged.

Ideal for an aquatic garden, this species has been cultivated for 3,000 years by the Chinese for its edible rhizomes and seeds (fox nuts), and the seeds are now sold in Indian markets roasted and 'puffed' like wheat.

Species, variety or cultivar:
–

Other common names:
Prickly water lily, Gorgon plant

Height and spread:
0.9 x 1.5 m (3 x 5 ft)

Blooming period:
Summer

Soil type:
–

Sun or Shade:
Needs full sun

Hardiness:
Minimum temp –12°C (10°F)

Eustoma grandiflorum • *Lisianthus*

DESCRIPTION

This genus, formerly classified as *Lianthus* and still sold under that name, has three species of annuals or short-lived perennials. *E. grandiflorum* is found from southern USA to Mexico, and has upright blue-green stems and fleshy, blue-green, pointed oval leaves, to 8 cm (3 in) long, and heads of bell-shaped flowers, to 6 cm (2½ in) across. There are many seedling strains, as well as individual named varieties, such as 'Forever Blue', which is 30 cm (12 in) tall, with large purple-blue flowers.

Slow-growing, they need prolonged warm conditions to flower well, and the heavy flower stems are best staked. Lisianthus means bitter flower, and refers to the taste; the flowers were used medicinally by Native Americans.

Species, variety or cultivar:
'Forever Blue'

Other common names:
Lisianthus, Prairie Gentian, Texas Bluebell

Height and spread:
30 x 30 cm (12 x 12 in)

Blooming period:
Summer

Soil type:
Fertile, moist, well-drained soil

Sun or Shade:
Likes full or half sun

Hardiness:
Minimum temp –7°C (20°F)

Exacum affine • *German Violet*

Species, variety or cultivar:
–

Other common names:
German Violet, Persian Violet

Height and spread:
45 x 30 cm (18 x 12 in)

Blooming period:
Spring through to autumn

Soil type:
A well-drained but moist potting mix

Sun or Shade:
Likes a well-lit position

Hardiness:
Minimum temp –1°C (30°F)

Description

A native of the island of Socotra at the mouth of the Red Sea, this annual or short-lived perennial has pointed oval leaves, and small fragrant flowers, ranging in colour from sky blue to pale and deep violet, which are borne from spring through to autumn.

Popular in temperate regions as pot plants for the house or conservatory, these plants can also be grown outdoors as a bedding annual, but are only really suitable for permanent outdoor cultivation in humid tropical and subtropical areas. Grow in a well-drained but moist potting mix in a well-lit position, and propagate from seed.

Felicia fruticosa

Description

This native to South Africa, although an evergreen shrub, is popular as an annual container and patio plant. It is advisable to place it in a greenhouse during winter in colder areas. The linear leaves are densely packed, and the ray florets are pink, purple or white, with a yellow disc. The fruits are hairy, and the lengthy flowering season through spring–summer can be extended by dead-heading.

They grow outdoors in moderately fertile soil, but prolonged damp conditions can kill them. In containers they need a loam-based compost with added grit for drainage.

Species, variety or cultivar:
–

Other common names:
–

Height and spread:
90 x 90 cm (36 x 36 in)

Blooming period:
Spring to summer

Soil type:
Moderately fertile soil

Sun or Shade:
Prefers full sun

Hardiness:
Minimum temp –7°C (20°F)

Gaillardia pulchella • *Blanket Flower*

Description

Discovered in the Rocky Mountains around 1825 by David Douglas, and named for a French patron, Gaillard de Charentonneau, this genus is comprised of around 30 species. The name blanket flower comes from a Native American legend of a blanket maker whom the spirits rewarded with an ever-blooming blanket of flowers on his grave.

G. pulchella is a hairy annual, found in northeastern Mexico and neighbouring parts of eastern and central USA. The leaves grow to over 8 cm (3 in) long, sometimes lobed and/or toothed. Flowerheads are around 6 cm (2½ in) wide, with ray florets yellow, red or red with yellow tips.

Species, variety or cultivar:

–

Other common names:

Blanket Flower, Firewheel

Height and spread:

60 x 40 cm (24 x 16 in)

Blooming period:

Summer to autumn

Soil type:

Gritty, well-drained soil that remains moist during the growing season

Sun or Shade:

Likes a sunny open position

Hardiness:

Minimum temp –12°C (10°F)

Gazania, hybrid cultivar • *Treasure Flower*

Species, variety or cultivar:
'Blackberry Ripple'
Other common names:
Treasure Flower
Height and spread:
15 x 50 cm (6 x 20 in)
Blooming period:
Summer
Soil type:
Gritty, very free-draining soil
Sun or Shade:
Likes a sunny open position
Hardiness:
Minimum temp –7°C (20°F)

Description

There are 16 species in this genus in the daisy (Asteraceae) family, found mainly in South Africa, with a few species extending the range to the tropics. Their flowers, which appear throughout the warmer months, are large, brightly coloured, often interestingly marked, and always showy.

Gazanias naturally flower in a wide range of colours and hybridize freely, so there is now a wide variety of garden forms, sizes and flower colours, such as 'Blackberry Ripple', which has buff ray florets, with a purple midstripe darkening towards the yellow disc.

Gazania rigens • *Treasure Flower*

Description

The name *Gazania* comes from Theodore of Gaza (1398–1478), who translated the botanical texts of *Theophrastus* from Greek into Latin. Gazanias are low, near-evergreen, clump-forming plants with simple, narrow, lance-shaped, sometimes downy leaves with paler undersides. While the species usually have yellow or orange flowers, garden forms are available in a huge colour range.

G. rigens has fleshy stems that strike root as they spread, forming large, leafy clumps. The leaves grow to over 10 cm (4 in) long, and are smooth-edged or near-pinnately lobed, deep green to bronze above, and white haired below. Long-stemmed flowerheads grow to 8 cm (3 in) wide, ray florets orange with a black base, and disc florets yellow or reddish orange. 'Variegata' has gold to orange flowers and foliage variegated with cream.

Apart from being somewhat frost tender and resenting wet winters, Gazanias are easily grown in any open sunny position with gritty very free-draining soil. They appreciate additional humus but will grow in poor dry soils. Propagate by division, or from basal cuttings or seed.

Species, variety or cultivar:
'Variegata'

Other common names:
Treasure Flower

Height and spread:
15 x 50 cm (6 x 20 in)

Blooming period:
Summer

Soil type:
Gritty, very free-draining soil

Sun or Shade:
Prefers an open position in full sun

Hardiness:
Minimum temp –7°C (20°F)

LEFT AND ABOVE RIGHT: Gazanias can add colour to the seaside garden, as they are extremely tolerant of coastal conditions. They open in full sun and close up during overcast weather and at dusk.

Gerbera • *Barberton Daisy*

Species, variety or cultivar:
Hybrid cultivar
Other common names:
Barberton Daisy, Transvaal Daisy
Height and spread:
45 x 30 cm (18 x 12 in)
Blooming period:
Spring to summer
Soil type:
Light, humus-rich soil, with added grit for drainage
Sun or Shade:
Likes half sun
Hardiness:
Minimum temp –7°C (20°F)

Description

The botanical name of this genus honours Traugott Gerber, a German botanist who travelled in Russia and died in 1743. Breeding of gerberas began at the end of the nineteenth century with the crossing of *G. jamesonii* and *G. viridiflora* in Cambridge, England. Most later cultivars are derived from this cross. Breeding was directed to producing long-stemmed blooms in a range of colours and varying degrees of doubleness, chiefly for the cut-flower industry, until short-stemmed seed-raised strains were developed for sale as flowering pot plants in the 1980s.

Gerberas are tender but can tolerate light frosts if kept barely moist in winter. Plant in full sun with deep, light, humus-rich soil with added grit for drainage. Popular as a houseplant and cut flower.

Gomphrena globosa • *Bachelor's Button*

DESCRIPTION

There are 90-odd species in this genus which is a part of the *amaranth* (Amaranthaceae) family. *G. globosa* originates from Panama and Guatemala, and is a bushy annual with slightly hairy pointed leaves. The flowers are papery and round, resembling a clover flower, and range from white through to red, purple and yellow, flowering in summer.

Outside the tropics these plants are treated as summer annuals, and they need long warm summers to flower well. Plant in moist humus-rich soil and water well, taking care not to overfeed, and propagate from seed.

Species, variety or cultivar:
Globosa

Other common names:
Bachelor's Button, Globe Amaranth

Height and spread:
60 x 45 cm (24 x 18 in)

Blooming period:
Summer

Soil type:
Moist, humus-rich soil

Sun or Shade:
Prefers full sun

Hardiness:
Minimum temp –18°C (0°F)

Gypsophila muralis • *Baby's Breath*

Description

Related to the pink (Caryophyllaceae) family, the 100-odd annuals and perennials in this genus occur naturally in temperate Eurasia. They can be spreading mat-forming plants studded with pink or white blooms, or upright shrubby species with billowing heads of tiny flowers.

G. muralis is a low spreading annual, which originates from central Europe to Siberia, and has narrow linear green to blue-green leaves. Billowing panicles densely packed with tiny white to mauve flowers appear in summer. 'Garden Bride' grows to 30 cm (12 in) tall, and has starry white and deep pink flowers.

Gypsophila means lime-loving, but most species are happy in any neutral to slightly alkaline soil that is fertile, moist and well-drained. Plant in full sun and propagate from basal cuttings or seed. The common name comes from the sweet scent of the flowers.

Species, variety or cultivar:
'Garden Bride'
Other common names:
Baby's Breath
Height and spread:
30 x 30 cm (12 x 12 in)
Blooming period:
Summer
Soil type:
Fertile, moist, well-drained soil
Sun or Shade:
Likes full to half sun
Hardiness:
Minimum temp –7°C (20°F)

ABOVE RIGHT AND FAR RIGHT: Not fussy about soil type, summer-flowering baby's breath will quickly fill bare areas of the garden where a burst of colour and speedy covering is required.

Gypsophila muralis • *Baby's Breath*

Description

G. muralis, originating from central Europe to Siberia, is a low spreading annual, and has narrow linear green to blue-green leaves. In summer, panicles densely packed with tiny white to mauve flowers form an appealing carpet of blooms. There are a number of attractive cultivars in the species, such as 'Gypsy', which is 30 cm (12 in) tall, and which forms a dense mound of flowing sprays of small, soft pink, double flowers.

Planted in any neutral to slightly alkaline soil that is fertile, moist and well-drained, this cultivar is an ideal addition to any rockery, or as a ground cover.

Species, variety or cultivar:
'Gypsy'

Other common names:
Baby's Breath

Height and spread:
30 x 30 cm (12 x 12 in)

Blooming period:
Summer

Soil type:
Fertile, moist, well-drained soil

Sun or Shade:
Likes full to half sun

Hardiness:
Minimum temp –7°C (20°F)

Hebe

Description

There are about 100 species in this genus in the figwort or foxglove (Scrophulariaceae) family, some from Australia and South America, but most native to New Zealand, such as *H. andersonii*, which is a hybrid of *H. speciosa* and *H. stricta*. This well-branched shrub has broadly lance-shaped leaves to 10 cm (4 in) long, and violet flowers crowded on spikes to 10 cm (4 in) long, which appear in summer through to autumn. 'Variegata' makes a colourful addition to the garden, with attractive foliage, in shades of dark green, greyish green and creamy white.

Species, variety or cultivar:
x andersonii 'Variegata'

Other common names:
–

Height and spread:
2 x 1.2 m (7 x 4 ft)

Blooming period:
Summer to autumn

Soil type:
Tolerates a wide range of soil conditions

Sun or Shade:
Prefers a sunny situation

Hardiness:
Minimum temp –7°C (20°F)

Helianthus annuus • *Common Sunflower*

Description

Sunflowers are so called not so much for the shape of the bloom as for the way the flowerhead turns to follow the sun. This genus of 70 annuals and perennials in the daisy (Asteraceae) family is from the Americas and is best known for the common or giant sunflower (*H. annuus*), an annual daisy that can grow to 5 m (17 ft) high. This species is widely grown commercially for its seeds and the oil extracted from them. Other species are smaller and tend to have lance-shaped rather than heart-shaped leaves. Most have bristly stems, and the flowers, nearly always yellow, are held above the foliage.

One of the many cultivars of *H. annuus* is 'Italian White', which grows to 1.5 m (5 ft) tall, and has very pale yellow flowers, darkening to gold towards the centre. Plant in a sunny, open position with fertile, moist, well-drained soil.

Species, variety or cultivar:
'Italian White'
Other common names:
Common Sunflower
Height and spread:
1.5 x 0.6 m (5 x 2 ft)
Blooming period:
Summer to early autumn
Soil type:
Fertile, moist, well-drained soil
Sun or Shade:
Needs full sun
Hardiness:
Minimum temp –34°C (–30°F)

FAR LEFT AND LEFT: Allergy sufferers will appreciate the pollenless sunflower cultivars that are now available, while birds will enjoy the nutritious seedheads that develop in the central disc.

Helianthus annuus • *Common Sunflower*

Description

This quick-growing annual is native to the USA, and has broad, bristly, toothed, pointed, heart-shaped leaves to 40cm (16 in) long, and flowerheads to 30 cm (12 in) wide, blooming from mid-summer through to autumn.

One of the many cultivars of this species is 'Ring of Fire', which grows to 1.5 m (5 ft) tall, and has flowers to 12 cm (5 in) wide, with striking golden-yellow and brick-red ray florets, from summer to early autumn. They should be planted in a sunny, open position with fertile, moist, well-drained soil, and propagation is from seed.

Species, variety or cultivar:'
'Ring of Fire'

Other common names:
Common Sunflower

Height and spread:
1.5 x 0.6 m (5 x 2 ft)

Blooming period:
Summer to early autumn

Soil type:
Fertile, moist, well-drained soil

Sun or Shade:
Needs full sun

Hardiness:
Minimum temp –34°C (–30°F)

Helianthus annuus • *Common Sunflower*

Species, variety or cultivar:
'Sunrich Orange'
Other common names:
Common Sunflower
Height and spread:
1.5 x 0.6 m (5 x 2 ft)
Blooming period:
Summer to early autumn
Soil type:
Fertile, moist, well-drained soil
Sun or Shade:
Needs full sun
Hardiness:
Minimum temp –34°C (–30°F)

Description

The best known Helianthus species is *H. annuus*, which is grown widely around the world for its seed and seed-oil. It is a quick-growing and spectacular species, native to the USA, and is the state flower of Kansas.

One of the many cultivars of *H. annuus* is 'Sunrich Orange', which grows to 1.5 m (5 ft) tall, and has bright golden yellow to orange ray florets, and no pollen. Plant this cultivar, as with most helianthus species, in a sunny, open position with fertile, moist, well-drained soil. Mildew can be a problem but usually only when the plants are past their best.

Helichrysum petiolare • *Liquorice Plant*

Description

This South African native is a spreading shrub that forms a mounding ground cover. It has a long soft stem and rounded leaves to over 3 cm (1¼ in) long. The leaves and stems are covered in a pale grey down, and small, dull white flowerheads are loosely clustered in winter. 'Limelight' is grown for its distinctive pale yellow-green foliage.

Most Helichrysum species are drought tolerant once established, and should be planted in full sun with light, gritty, very well-drained soil. Their frost hardiness varies, but few will tolerate prolonged cold. Any trimming or shaping should be done in spring.

Species, variety or cultivar:
'Limelight'
Other common names:
Liquorice Plant
Height and spread:
0.45 x 1.5 m (18 x 60 in)
Blooming period:
Winter
Soil type:
Light, gritty, very well-drained soil
Sun or Shade:
Prefers full sun
Hardiness:
Minimum temp –7°C (20°F)

Heliotropium arborescens • *Cherry Pie*

Description

A member of the borage (Boraginaceae) family, this is a genus of about 250 species, mainly evergreen shrubs, from Central America and temperate South America. Some species are locally important for medicinal purposes, and others are significant ornamentals.

H. arborescens comes from tropical Peru, and is a spreading, evergreen bun-shaped shrub with narrow oval leaves, dark and shiny above, and paler on their reverse. Abundant sweetly perfumed mauve to purple flowers appear from early spring to late summer. The species prefers fertile free-draining soils, summer moisture and shelter from the cold, with full sun to filtered light being the favoured habitat.

Species, variety or cultivar:
–

Other common names:
Cherry Pie, Common Heliotrope

Height and spread:
0.9 x 0.5 m (36 x 20 in)

Blooming period:
Spring and summer

Soil type:
Fertile, free-draining soils

Sun or Shade:
Full sun to filtered light

Hardiness:
Minimum temp –7°C (20°F)

Heliotropium arborescens • *Cherry Pie*

Description

H. arborescens, a native to tropical Peru, has a number of cultivars, all of which are good for use in borders or pots. 'Fragrant Delight', a spreading shrub with narrow oval leaves that are lighter on their underside than on top, has striking dark purple flowers, which are strongly scented, and which appear in profusion from early spring to late summer. Where frosts occur, the most sheltered position in the garden must be selected, and a fertile, free-draining soil in full sun to filtered light is ideal.

Species, variety or cultivar:
'Fragrant Delight'

Other common names:
Cherry Pie, Common Heliotrope

Height and spread:
0.9 x 0.5 m (36 x 20 in)

Blooming period:
Spring and summer

Soil type:
Fertile, free-draining soils

Sun or Shade:
Full sun to filtered light

Hardiness:
Minimum temp –7°C (20°F)

Heliotropium arborescens • *Cherry Pie*

Species, variety or cultivar:
'Lord Roberts'

Other common names:
Cherry Pie, Common Heliotrope

Height and spread:
0.9 x 0.5 m (36 x 20 in)

Blooming period:
Spring and summer

Soil type:
Fertile, free-draining soils

Sun or Shade:
Full sun to filtered light

Hardiness:
Minimum temp –7°C (20°F)

Description

A cultivar of the Peruvian *H. arborescens*, 'Lord Roberts' is characterized by compact growth and clusters of violet flowers, which appear in copious numbers from early spring to late summer. Like other cultivars of *H. arborescens*, 'Lord Roberts' makes a great ornamental, and is suitable for use in both borders and pots.

As with similar cultivars, where frosts occur, the most sheltered position in the garden must be selected, and a fertile, free-draining soil in full sun to filtered light is ideal. Prune moderately to encourage new shoots, and propagate from soft-tip cuttings in spring or summer or half-hardened cuttings in autumn to winter in a warm and moist situation.

Hibiscus moscheutos • *Common Rose Mallow*

Description

This genus of over 200 annual or perennial herbs, shrubs, or trees, is in the mallow (Malvaceae) family, and is widely distributed throughout warm-temperate, subtropical and tropical regions of the world. They are grown mostly for their large dramatic flowers, borne singly or in terminal clusters, usually lasting for just one day. The open bell-shaped flowers appear in a wide range of colours, and are characterized by a prominent staminal column and a darker colouring in the centre. The alternate leaves are usually palmate, and the fruit is a capsule.

H. moscheutos is from eastern North America, and is common from Ohio through to Alabama and Florida. This species has lobed leaves, 5–15 cm (2–6 in) long, and large trumpet-shaped flowers in pink and white produced from spring to summer. 'Lord Baltimore' has large, single, crimson red flowers that are quite striking.

Species, variety or cultivar:
'Lord Baltimore'
Other common names:
Common Rose Mallow, Swamp Rose Mallow
Height and spread:
2.4 x 0.1 m (60 x 40 in)
Blooming period:
Spring to summer
Soil type:
A rich and moist soil
Sun or Shade:
Prefers full sun
Hardiness:
Minimum temp –29°C (–20°F)

LEFT AND ABOVE: Hibiscus species are usually easy to grow, but they do need a warm position and regular watering and feeding during the growing season. To keep the plant shape, trim after flowering.

Hibiscus mutabilis • *Confederate Rose*

Description

This species of hibiscus is a native of China, and is a small, spreading deciduous shrub, or erect, branching small tree. Large palm-shaped leaves have seven serrated lobes, and large double or single flowers, white or pink with a darker base and staminal column, and appear in summer. 'Plena' is a cultivar with rounded double summer- to autumn-blooming flowers that open white or light pink and turn a deep rose red as they age. Drought tender and rather frost tender, they prefer a position in full sun in a rich moist soil.

Species, variety or cultivar:
'Plena'

Other common names:
Confederate Rose, Cotton Rose

Height and spread:
4.5 x 2.4 m (15 x 8 ft)

Blooming period:
Late summer to autumn

Soil type:
Rich moist soil

Sun or Shade:
Likes full sun

Hardiness:
Minimum temp –12°C (10°F)

Hunnemannia fumariifolia • *Golden Cup*

Species, variety or cultivar:
–
Other common names:
Golden Cup, Mexican Tulip Poppy
Height and spread:
90 x 25 cm (36 x 10 in)
Blooming period:
Summer
Soil type:
Well-drained soil
Sun or Shade:
Likes full sun
Hardiness:
Minimum temp –12°C (10°F)

Description

This genus belongs to the poppy (Papaveraceae) family and contains only one species, which is often grown as an annual. It is native to highland areas of Mexico, and although woody at the base, it is of delicate appearance with finely divided bluish grey foliage. The satiny flowers are clearest yellow, up to 3 cm (3 in) wide, and are held above the foliage in summer.

Grow in full sun in a well-drained soil, as it will not tolerate wet conditions. Care should be taken not to disturb the roots on transplanting, and propagate from seed.

Hypoestes aristata • *Ribbon Bush*

Description

This genus of 40 species is found in open woodland regions of South Africa, Madagascar and Southeast Asia. *H. aristata* is an evergreen shrubby plant with downy mid-green leaves held opposite on upright stems and masses of small purple flowers in the upper leaf axils, appearing in autumn. Grow in humus-enriched well-drained soil, watering freely in summer, but keeping drier in the cold months when growth is not apparent. These half-hardy plants do well in part-shade with protection from drying winds. Propagate in spring from seed, or from stem cuttings taken from spring to summer, and prune after flowering.

Species, variety or cultivar:
–

Other common names:
Ribbon Bush

Height and spread:
90 x 65 cm (36 x 26 in)

Blooming period:
Autumn

Soil type:
Humus-enriched well-drained soil

Sun or Shade:
Prefers half sun

Hardiness:
Minimum temp –7°C (20°F)

Iberis umbellata • *Candytuft*

Description

Popular for the bold effect of their massed heads of white, pink, mauve or purple flowers, the 30-odd annuals, perennials and subshrubs in this genus in the cabbage (Brassicaceae) family are found from western and southern Europe to western Asia.

I. umbellata is an annual from southern Europe, has very narrow lance-shaped leaves that are sometimes toothed, and produces purple flowers from spring to summer. The flower colours of Flash Mixed Series include white, all shades of pink, mauve, red and purple. Grow from autumn-sown seed in mild areas, and dead-head regularly to encourage continuous blooming.

Species, variety or cultivar:
Flash Mixed cultivar

Other common names:
Candytuft

Height and spread:
30 x 40 cm (12 x 16 in)

Blooming period:
Spring and summer

Soil type:
Light yet moist, well-drained soil

Sun or Shade:
Enjoys half to full sun

Hardiness:
Minimum temp –18°C (0°F)

Impatiens • *Busy Lizzie*

Description

The type genus giving its name to the balsam (Balsaminaceae) family is home to around 850 species of annuals, perennials and subshrubs found worldwide except in Australasia, South America and the polar regions. These are generally soft-stemmed plants with simple, pointed, lance-shaped leaves, often with toothed edges. Flowers appear through the year in mild areas and have five petals, an upper standard and the lower four fused into two pairs, the sepals also partly fused to form a spur. When ripe, the seedpods explosively eject their contents at the slightest touch, hence the genus name from the Latin for 'impatient'.

New Guinea Hybrids are usually cultivars of *I. hawkeri* or hybrids with *I. linearifolia*. They generally resemble *I. hawkeri* but are available in many striking combinations of flower and foliage, such as 'Celebrette Hot Pink', which has vivid magenta flowers and mid-green leaves.

Species, variety or cultivar:
New Guinea, 'Celebrette Hot Pink'
Other common names:
Balsam, Busy Lizzie, Water Fuchsia
Height and spread:
120 x 100 cm (48 x 40 in)
Blooming period:
Summer to autumn
Soil type:
Deep, cool, moist, humus-rich soil
Sun or Shade:
Likes half sun to full shade
Hardiness:
Minimum temp –1°C (30°F)

ABOVE RIGHT: *New Guinea 'Danziger Salmon'*
Most *Impatiens* species make great indoor specimens, either in pots or hanging baskets. Keep the soil moist and tip prune to encourage more compact growth. You can also enjoy the showy leaves and jewel-like flowers in beds, borders and containers.

Impatiens • *Busy Lizzie*

DESCRIPTION

Usually cultivars of *I. hawkeri* or hybrids with *I. linearifolia*, and generally resembling *I. hawkeri*, New Guinea Hybrids are available in many attractive combinations of flower and foliage. 'Timor' is a good example of such a combination, with deep orange-red flowers, and red-tinted bright green leaves.

They can be grown as summer plants in cooler climates outside the recommended zones, provided they are given shade from the hottest sun and planted in deep, cool, moist, humus-rich soil. Feed well and propagate from seed. Keep an eye on the plants, as they self-sow and can sometimes become slightly invasive.

Species, variety or cultivar:
New Guinea, 'Timor'

Other common names:
Balsam, Busy Lizzie, Water Fuchsia

Height and spread:
120 x 100 cm (48 x 40 in)

Blooming period:
Summer to autumn

Soil type:
Cool, moist, humus-rich soil

Sun or Shade:
Likes half sun to full shade

Hardiness:
Minimum temp –1°C (30°F)

Impatiens walleriana • *Busy Lizzie*

Species, variety or cultivar:
Fiesta Series, 'Salmon Sunrise'

Other common names:
Balsam, Busy Lizzie, Water Fuchsia

Height and spread:
60 x 50 cm (24 x 20 in)

Blooming period:
Summer to autumn

Soil type:
Deep, cool, moist, humus-rich soil

Sun or Shade:
Likes half sun to full shade

Hardiness:
Minimum temp –1°C (30°F)

Description

This species of *impatiens* is a continuous-flowering, shrubby, evergreen, tropical east African perennial, often treated as an annual. Fleshy, succulent stems support toothed lance-shaped leaves, which are often red-tinted. Spurred flat-faced flowers, with evenly sized petals, occur in most colours except yellow and blue.

I. walleriana has numerous cultivars and seedling strains, including the Fiesta Series, which is characterized by rosebud double flowers in many shades including bicolours. 'Salmon Sunrise' is a member of this series, and produces masses of attractive dark salmon-pink double flowers throughout summer. They can be moved indoors after the growing season to a sunny position.

Impatiens walleriana • *Busy Lizzie*

Description

Often treated as an annual, *I. walleriana* is a continuous-flowering, shrubby, evergreen, from tropical east Africa. Fleshy, succulent stems support toothed lance-shaped leaves, which are often red-tinted. Spurred flat-faced flowers, with evenly sized petals, occur in most colours except yellow and blue.

One of the numerous cultivars and seedling strains of *I. walleriana* is the Super Elfin Series, which is characterized by its single flowers in a range of colours, as well as by its compact habit. 'Blue Pearl', a member of this series, is a small compact shrub, which is covered with abundant dainty light pink flowers throughout summer. They can be moved indoors after the growing season to a sunny position.

Provided they are given shade from the hottest sun and planted in deep, cool, moist, humus-rich soil, these can be grown as summer plants in cooler climates outside the recommended zones. They self-sow and can sometimes become slightly invasive.

LEFT AND ABOVE: This half-hardy annual is a standard for summer shade gardens. The thick, decorative foliage is covered with a profusion of blooms. Flowers come in a wide range of bright colours. Impatiens enjoy infrequent feeding with a balanced fertilizer. Let the soil dry out just a bit between waterings to encourage compact growth and profuse flowering. Start seeds indoors six to eight weeks before the last frost. The plant makes an attractive hanging basket.

Species, variety or cultivar:
Super Elfin Series, 'Blue Pearl'

Other common names:
Balsam, Busy Lizzie, Water Fuchsia

Height and spread:
60 x 50 cm (24 x 20 in)

Blooming period:
Summer to autumn

Soil type:
Deep, cool, moist, humus-rich soil

Sun or Shade:
Likes half sun to full shade

Hardiness:
Minimum temp –1°C (30°F)

Impatiens walleriana • *Busy Lizzie*

Description

The cultivar 'Victoria Rose' of the tropical east Africa species *I. walleriana* has fleshy, succulent stems that support toothed lance-shaped leaves, and spurred flat-faced flowers, which have deep pink evenly sized petals. It grows up to 50 cm (24 in) high, with a spreading habit to 50 cm (20 in) across, and as with all impatiens, this plant should be provided with shade from the hottest sun, and planted in deep, cool, moist, humus-rich soil. Water well, and propagate from seed. Keep an eye on the plants, as they self-sow and can sometimes become slightly invasive.

Species, variety or cultivar:
'Victoria Rose'

Other common names:
Balsam, Busy Lizzie, Water Fuchsia

Height and spread:
60 x 50 cm (24 x 20 in)

Blooming period:
Summer to autumn

Soil type:
Deep, cool, moist, humus-rich soil

Sun or Shade:
Likes half sun to full shade

Hardiness:
Minimum temp –1°C (30°F)

Ipomoea batatas • *Kumara*

DESCRIPTION

This large and variable genus in the bindweed (Convolvulaceae) family, takes its name from the Greek word for a type of worm, because many of its members are twining climbers; others are annual or perennial herbs, shrubs and small trees.

I. batatas is native to tropical regions, where it is an important food crop with edible tubers, which have purple, red or yellow skins. It is usually grown as a prostrate annual, and has leaves that are oval to heart-shaped, lobed or toothed. 'Vardaman' has ornamental dark green foliage, flushed purple when young, and orange-fleshed tubers.

Species, variety or cultivar:
'Vardaman'

Other common names:
Kumara, Sweet Potato

Height and spread:
3 x 3 m (10 x 10 ft)

Blooming period:
Summer to autumn

Soil type:
Fertile, well-drained soil

Sun or Shade:
Needs full sun

Hardiness:
Minimum temp –7°C (20°F)

Ipomoea indica • *Blue Dawn Flower*

Description

This genus is widely cultivated in tropical to warm-temperate areas for their vigorous growth and showy flowers that appear in the leaf axils and range from bell-shaped to tubular. *Ipomoea* species prefer full sun and plenty of water in the growing season but will make the best of almost any conditions.

I. indica is found throughout tropical regions, and is a vigorous climber regarded as a nuisance weed in some areas. The species has broadly heart-shaped leaves and funnel-shaped flowers, produced throughout the year, which open dark blue or purple, occasionally white, and fade throughout the day.

Species, variety or cultivar:
–

Other common names:
Blue Dawn Flower, Morning Glory

Height and spread:
9 x 9 m (30 x 30 ft)

Blooming period:
Spring to autumn

Soil type:
Fertile, well-drained soil

Sun or Shade:
Likes full sun

Hardiness:
Minimum temp –7°C (20°F)

Ipomoea mauritiana

Description

A species from this large and variable genus from the bindweed (Convolvulaceae) family, *I. mauritiana* is a vigorous woody climber found throughout the tropics. With palm-like, 3–9 lobed leaves, it has funnel to bell-shaped pink to maroon flowers that are darkest in colour at the base of the corolla, and which appear in the leaf axils in summer.

Useful for covering fences or trellises, this species can also be grown in pots, and likes full sun and plenty of water in the growing season.

Species, variety or cultivar:
–

Other common names:
–

Height and spread:
4.5 x 1.8 m (15 x 6 ft)

Blooming period:
Summer

Soil type:
Fertile, well-drained soil

Sun or Shade:
Enjoys full sun

Hardiness:
Minimum temp –7°C (20°F)

Ipomoea x multifida • *Cardinal flower*

Description

A member of the bindweed (Convolvulaceae) family, the large and variable genus Ipomoea takes its name from the Greek word for a type of worm, because many of its members are twining climbers; others are annual or perennial herbs, shrubs and small trees. They are widely cultivated in tropical to warm-temperature areas for their showy flowers and vigorous growth. Some species, including the sweet potato (*I. batatus*), have tuberous roots that are used as food. Flowers appear in the leaf axils and range from bell-shaped to tubular.

I. x multifida is of garden origin, and is a hybrid of *I. coccinea* and *I. quamoclit*. Its leaves are deeply divided, with several linear lobes. Funnel-shaped flowers, 2.5–5 cm (1–2 in) wide, red with white centres, appear from summer to autumn. They prefer full sun and plenty of water in the growing season but will make the best of almost any conditions. Make sure these plants have plenty of room and cut back after flowering. They may require support.

LEFT AND BELOW: The genus is notable for easy culture, quick growth and beautiful bell-shaped to tubular flowers appearing in colours ranging from purple through red to blue, white or yellow.

Species, variety or cultivar:
x multifida
Other common names:
Cardinal Flower
Height and spread:
3 x 1.8 m (10 x 6 ft)
Blooming period:
Summer to fall
Soil type:
Fertile, well-drained soil
Sun or Shade:
Needs full shade
Hardiness:
Minimum temp –12°C (10°F)

Ipomoea tricolor • *Morning Glory*

Description

This Ipomoea species, from Mexico and South America, is an annual climber with heart-shaped leaves. Wide funnel-shaped flowers that are sky blue, with a yellow interior and base, appear in summer and fade as the day progresses. 'Tie Dye' is a cultivar with interesting leaves of green, purple and white, contrasting, as the name suggests, in a similar way to tie-dyed material. *I. tricolor*'s climbing habit makes this species suitable for covering fences or trellises. Make sure it has plenty of room and cut back after flowering.

Species, variety or cultivar:
'Tie Dye'

Other common names:
Morning Glory

Height and spread:
3 x 0.9 m (10 x 3 ft)

Blooming period:
Summer

Soil type:
Fertile, well-drained soil

Sun or Shade:
Likes full sun

Hardiness:
Minimum temp –12°C (10°F)

Lathyrus odoratus • *Sweet Pea*

Description

This genus in the pea-flower subfamily of the legume (Fabaceae) family has far more than just the old-fashioned and popular sweet peas to offer among its 110 species of annuals and perennials.

L. odoratus comes from Italy and the Mediterranean islands, and is a highly scented annual climber with angled, somewhat downy stems and paired blue-green leaflets, to over 5 cm (2 in) long. Among its many cultivars is 'All But Blue' which has the faintest lilac-tinted white petals with a fine mauve-pink border. Grow in a sunny well-ventilated position.

Species, variety or cultivar:
'All But Blue'

Other common names:
Sweet Pea

Height and spread:
2.4 x 0.1 m (96 x 40 in)

Blooming period:
Summer

Soil type:
Moist, well-drained soil

Sun or Shade:
Full or half sun

Hardiness:
Minimum temp –12°C (10°F)

Lathyrus odoratus • *Sweet Pea*

Description

This genus has more than 110 species of annuals and perennials, and is found in Eurasia, North America, temperate South America and the mountains of East Africa. Many are climbers, others are low-spreading plants, and some are shrubby.

L. odoratus is from Italy and the Mediterranean islands, and the wild species has racemes of up to three violet and purple red flowers in summer. Garden forms are heavier flowering in a very wide range of colours. 'Eclipse' displays masses of deep lavender to pink flowers in summer, and likes a well-ventilated sunny spot.

Species, variety or cultivar:
'Eclipse'

Other common names:
Sweet Pea

Height and spread:
2.4 x 0.1 m (96 x 40 in)

Blooming period:
Summer

Soil type:
Moist, well-drained soil

Sun or Shade:
Full or half sun

Hardiness:
Minimum temp –12°C (10°F)

Lathyrus odoratus • *Sweet Pea*

Species, variety or cultivar:
'Mollie Rilstone'
Other common names:
Sweet Pea
Height and spread:
2.4 x 0.1 m (96 x 40 in)
Blooming period:
Summer
Soil type:
Moist, well-drained soil
Sun or Shade:
Full or half sun
Hardiness:
Minimum temp –12°C (10°F)

Description

This species from Italy and the Mediterranean islands should be planted in moist well-drained soil, with a stake or wire for it to climb. Propagate from seed sown in early spring, or in autumn–winter in mild climates. Although the wild species has violet and purple red flowers, garden forms are heavier flowering in a wide variety of colours. One of many cultivars of *L. odoratus*, 'Mollie Rilstone' has creamy petals, the upper petal with a blush of pink, and prefers full sun, in a well-ventilated position to lessen the risk of botrytis.

Lathyrus odoratus • *Sweet Pea*

Description

Found in Eurasia, North America, temperate South America and the mountains of East Africa, this genus of 110 species in the legume (Fabaceae) family is comprised of climbers, low-spreading and shrubby plants. The climbers support themselves with tendrils growing at the tips of the pinnate leaves, where the terminal leaflet would be. The typical pea-flowers occur in many colours, and may be borne singly or in racemes arising from the upper leaf axils.

L. odoratus is a highly-scented annual climber originating in the Mediterranean islands and Italy, and has paired blue-green leaflets, to over 5 cm (2 in) long, on somewhat downy stems. The heavy-flowering garden forms occur in a wide range of colours, such as 'Winner', which has masses of attractive red flowers suffused with orange, borne in summer. Sow in autumn in temperate climates, or in spring in cooler climates, in sunny well-ventilated conditions.

LEFT AND BELOW: *Lathyrus* comes from the Greek name *lathyros* meaning pea or pulse which in turn is a combination of *la-*, *very* and *thoures*, a stimulant, as the seeds were said to have excitant or irritant properties.

Species, variety or cultivar:
'Winner'

Other common names:
Sweet Pea

Height and spread:
2.4 x 0.1 m (96 x 40 in)

Blooming period:
Summer

Soil type:
Moist, well-drained soil

Sun or Shade:
Full or half sun

Hardiness:
Minimum temp –12°C (10°F)

Lavatera arborea • *Tree Mallow*

DESCRIPTION

There are 25 species in this genus within the mallow (Malvaceae) family found from the Mediterranean to the northwest Himalayas, and in parts of Asia, Australia, California, USA and Baja California, Mexico. The leaves are usually palmately lobed and slightly downy, and most species have attractive hibiscus-like flowers with prominent staminal columns, in colours ranging from white to a rosy purple.

L. arborea is from Europe and the Mediterranean region, and is naturalized in California, USA and Baja California, Mexico. The leaves are large, lobed, soft and velvety, and purplish red flowers with darker veins appear in early summer. 'Variegata' has attractive leaves marbled with creamy white.

This type of shrubby mallow is suitable for planting in mixed borders, where it will bloom abundantly throughout the summer, provided it is grown in full sun in light well-drained soil. Prune after flowering and propagate by softwood cuttings taken in spring or early summer.

Species, variety or cultivar:
'Variegata'

Other common names:
Tree Mallow

Height and spread:
3 x 1.8 m (10 x 6 ft)

Blooming period:
Early summer

Soil type:
Light, well-drained soil

Sun or Shade:
Sun or shade

Hardiness:
Minimum temp –12°C (10°F)

Lavatera trimestis • *Annual Mallow*

Description

From the Mediterranean region, this species is a bushy easy-to-grow annual that does not need to be staked. 'Ruby Regis' has silk cup-shaped cerise pink flowers, and grows to 60 cm (24 in) tall. Suitable for planting in mixed borders, where they will bloom abundantly throughout summer, they should be grown in full sun in light, well-drained soil. Too rich a soil will result in an excess of foliage at the expense of flowers, and plants should be pruned after flowering to prevent legginess. Softwood cuttings taken in spring or early summer strike readily and are the usual method of propagation.

Species, variety or cultivar:
'Ruby Regis'

Other common names:
Annual Mallow, Regal Mallow, Rose Mallow, Royal Mallow

Height and spread:
1.2 x 0.9 m (48 x 36 in)

Blooming period:
Summer

Soil type:
Light, well-drained soil

Sun or Shade:
Enjoys half sun

Hardiness:
Minimum temp –12°C (10°F)

Leonotis nepetifolia • *Lion's Ear*

Species, variety or cultivar:
–
Other common names:
Annual Lion's Ear, Lion's Ear
Height and spread:
1.2 x 0.3 m (48 x 12 in)
Blooming period:
Late summer to winter
Soil type:
Moderately fertile soil
Sun or Shade:
Needs full sun
Hardiness:
Minimum temp –12°C (10°F)

Description

From India and Africa, and now naturalized in parts of North America, this annual has opposite pairs of serrated mid-green leaves to 12 cm (5 in) long, borne on upright squarish stems. In late summer to winter, whorls of narrow orange trumpet flowers are arranged densely about the stems. These are warm-climate plants that can be grown under cover in frost-prone areas. They need moderately fertile soil in full sun and ample water in the growing season. The somewhat brittle stems can be cut back in spring. Propagate from seed or from softwood cuttings in summer.

Annual Lion's Ear was originally native to tropical and subtropical Africa, as are the 30 other species in the genus. However, it is now naturalized all over the world in appropriate climates, where it grows along road shoulders, in abandoned fields and in disturbed areas. Annual Lion's Ear occurs throughout Florida and much of the American south.

Limonium sinuatum • *Sea Lavender*

DESCRIPTION

Native to the Mediterranean, this summer-flowering perennial is often short-lived and treated as an annual. All parts are downy, and the leaves are pinnately lobed, lance-shaped, and 2.5–10 cm (1–4 in) long. The flower stems are winged, with many short compact spikes of papery flowers, and the wild species has lavender, pink or white flowers.

This species has a preference for sheltered sunny locations and light, well-drained, yet moist soil. If the flowers are not cut for indoor use, they should be removed, as allowing the plants to set seed can shorten their life.

Species, variety or cultivar:
–

Other common names:
Sea Lavender, Statice

Height and spread:
40 x 40 cm (16 x 16 in)

Blooming period:
Summer to early autumn

Soil type:
Light, well-drained, moist soil

Sun or Shade:
Likes a sunny location

Hardiness:
Minimum temp –7°C (20°F)

Linaria maroccana • *Annual Toadflax*

Description

From the foxglove (Scrophulariaceae) family, this genus encompasses about 150 species of annuals and perennials found in Europe (mainly around the Mediterranean) and temperate Asia. Toadflaxes are closely related to snapdragons, with similar but smaller flowers, and are easy to cultivate but stop flowering in hot weather. For best effect, plant in masses, as the individual plants are wispy. The name is derived from the Greek *linon*, flax, because of the similarity in foliage.

L. maroccana is from Morocco, is naturalized in northeastern USA, and has alternate, narrow, grass-like leaves. Profuse tiny snapdragon-like flowers in white, yellow, pink, red and dark blue to purple shades appear in early summer.

Species, variety or cultivar:
–

Other common names:
Annual Toadflax, Bunny Rabbits, Morocco

Height and spread:
25 x 30 cm (10 x 12 in)

Blooming period:
Summer

Soil type:
Well-drained soil

Sun or Shade:
Likes full sun

Hardiness:
Minimum temp –7°C (20°F)

Linum grandiflorum • *Scarlet Flax*

DESCRIPTION

This genus comprises about 180 species and is native to temperate or subtropical regions of the world, though predominately from the Northern hemisphere. They are delicate but easy-to-grow plants, with stems that are erect and branching and simple, narrow, grey-green leaves. The cup-shaped to funnel-shaped 5-petalled flowers are carried in branched clusters at the stem tips, lasting only one day, but they are produced in great numbers throughout the summer.

L. grandiflorum is from Algeria and has slender stems with narrow, pointed, pale green leaves and single, saucer-shaped flowers, 3.5 cm (1½ in) across, in early–late summer. 'Rubrum' has tall, brilliant crimson flowers.

Species, variety or cultivar:
'Rubrum'

Other common names:
Flowering Flax, Scarlet Flax

Height and spread:
30 x 30 cm (12 x 12 in)

Blooming period:
Summer

Soil type:
Well-drained humus-rich soil

Sun or Shade:
Enjoys full sun

Hardiness:
Minimum temp –18°C (0°F)

Lithodora diffusa

Description

This species is from France, Spain and Portugal, and is a creeping plant with green linear leaves and small vibrant blue flowers that appear in late spring or early summer. With age, it tends to stop producing foliage and flowers in the centre. 'Star' has petals edged with clear white, giving a starry appearance.

The low-growing habit makes these ideal for ground covers, rockeries or at the front of borders. Grow in well-drained acid soil in full sun to partial shade, as they can become leggy in too much shade. Propagate from seed in spring or from tip cuttings in mid- to late summer.

Species, variety or cultivar:
'Star'

Other common names:
–

Height and spread:
30 x 90 cm (12 x 36 in)

Blooming period:
Spring to summer

Soil type:
Well-drained acid soil

Sun or Shade:
Likes both full sun and part shade

Hardiness:
Minimum temp –18°C (0°F)

Lobelia erinus • *Bedding Lobelia*

Description

This small, long-flowering, South African perennial is usually treated as an annual, and has a dense mounding habit, fine stems and small, often purple-tinted, deep green leaves, which are roughly oval and toothed. Masses of small pale-centered 5-lobed flowers, the lower 3 lobes enlarged, in blue, mauve and purple, appear in summer. There are a number of seedling strains that differ mainly in size and growth habit.

Lobelia species were used medicinally by Native Americans, and the Cherokee of the eighteenth century reputedly had an infallible lobelia-based cure for syphilis. The plants prefer a sunny position with moist well-drained soil.

Species, variety or cultivar:
–

Other common names:
Bedding Lobelia, Edging Lobelia

Height and spread:
20 x 40 cm (8 x 16 in)

Blooming period:
Summer

Soil type:
Moist, well-drained soil

Sun or Shade:
Prefers a sunny position

Hardiness:
Minimum temp –7°C (20°F)

Lobularia maritima • *Bedding Lobelia*

Description

This genus of five species in the cabbage (Brassicaceae) family is from the northern temperate zones, and is characterized by small mounding plants with simple linear to lance-shaped leaves, sometimes with fine silvery hairs. Tiny, often sweet-scented flowers appear in the warmer months, in rounded heads.

L. maritima is widespread in northern temperate zones, and is an annual or short-lived perennial, which forms a compact mound of narrow dull green leaves, about 2.5 cm (1 in) long. Tiny flowers in massed rounded heads are usually white to cream, and there are garden forms in several sizes and colours.

Species, variety or cultivar:
–

Other common names:
Bedding Lobelia, Edging Lobelia

Height and spread:
25 x 40 cm (10 x 16 in)

Blooming period:
Spring to summer

Soil type:
Light, free-draining soil

Sun or Shade:
Likes full sun

Hardiness:
Minimum temp –18°C (0°F)

Malcomia maritima • *Virginia Stock*

Description

This genus has some 35 species and is found from Europe to Afghanistan. Mainly small mounding plants, the foliage is variably shaped but often finely hairy and with toothed edges. The purplish red, often fragrant flowers are 4-petalled, in open racemes.

M. maritima is an annual native to Greece and Albania, with upright branching stems, and hairy, 5 cm (2 in) long, elliptical, smooth-edged or toothed, leaves. Racemes of fragrant pinkish purple flowers, to 2.5 cm (1 in) wide, appear in spring–summer. Plant in full sun with free-draining soil that can be kept moist, and avoid over-feeding, which can result in very few flowers.

Species, variety or cultivar:
–

Other common names:
Virginia Stock

Height and spread:
35 x 30 cm (14 x 12 in)

Blooming period:
Spring to summer

Soil type:
Free-draining soil that can be kept moist

Sun or Shade:
Prefers full sun

Hardiness:
Minimum temp –12°C (10°F)

Matthiola incana • *Brompton Stock*

Species, variety or cultivar:
Vintage Series, 'Vintage Burgundy'
Other common names:
Brompton Stock
Height and spread:
20 x 20 cm (8 x 8 in)
Blooming period:
Summer
Soil type:
Moist, well-drained soil
Sun or Shade:
Likes full sun
Hardiness:
Minimum temp –12°C (10°F)

Description

From southern and western Europe, this species has grey-green, downy, 5 cm (2 in) long elliptical leaves, and upright spikes of scented purple, pink or white 4-petalled flowers, which appear in summer. The Vintage Series is characterized by branching examples, in most colours, many of them double, and members of this series, such as 'Vintage Burgundy' are named for the colour of their blooms.

Famed for their scent, stocks were once grown for medicinal purposes and a comment attributed to Italian botanist Pierandrea Mattioli, after whom the genus is named, that he grew stock only for 'matters of love and lust', suggests the medicine had much to do with the scent.

Melampodium leucanthum • *Blackfoot Daisy*

DESCRIPTION

The 37 annual or perennial herbs and subshrubs in this genus from the daisy (Asteraceae) family are native to the warmer parts of North America and Mexico. They have narrow to oval-toothed or simple leaves, and carry heads of daisy-like flowers with white to pale yellow ray florets and yellow disc florets. These plants are suited to a sunny position in moist well-drained soil. During winter reduce the amount of water given.

M. leucanthum is short-lived and mound-forming, and is found from Mexico to Colorado, USA. Its leaves, 5 cm (2 in) long, are smooth or divided into six lobes, and honey-scented flowerheads, with white to cream ray florets, appear in spring–autumn. They are reasonably tolerant of both drought and poor soil, provided it is loose enough to cope with the plant's taproot. Not suited to division, or to transplanting, this species can be propagated from seed.

Species, variety or cultivar:
–
Other common names:
Blackfoot Daisy
Height and spread:
60 x 60 cm (24 x 24 in)
Blooming period:
Spring to autumn
Soil type:
Moist, well-drained soil
Sun or Shade:
Likes full sun
Hardiness:
Minimum temp –34°C (–30°F)

ABOVE AND RIGHT: The leaves of the Blackfoot Daisy have rough hairs and are 2.5–5 cm (1–2 in) in length. The flowerhead consists of 7 to 13 white ray flowers and 25 to 50 yellow disc flowers and blooms from April to October. The leaves and flowers are readily eaten by white-tailed deer and also attract butterflies.

Melampodium paludosum • *Butter Daisy*

DESCRIPTION

Part of the daisy (Asteraceae) family, this annual herb is native to Mexico, and has light green oblong leaves on purplish green stems. Masses of solitary, yellow, daisy-like flowers, with darker centres, appear in late spring to early autumn, and may self-sow in suitable conditions. 'Showstar' has golden yellow daisy-like flowers, suited to a sunny position in moist well-drained soil. Less water should be given in winter to this plant, which can be propagated from seed, and its appearance and habit make it an ideal choice for rockeries, or for sunny banks.

Species, variety or cultivar:
'Showstar'

Other common names:
Butter Daisy, Gold Medallion Flower

Height and spread:
60 x 90 cm (24 x 36 in)

Blooming period:
Spring to autumn

Soil type:
Moist, well-drained soil

Sun or Shade:
Prefers full sun

Hardiness:
Minimum temp 4°C (40°F)

Mesembryanthemum guerichianum

Description

This genus contains 40 to 50 species of prostrate or creeping succulents in the iceplant (Aizoaceae) family, and is native to South Africa and Namibia. All parts of the plant are covered with tiny glandular hairs, and rosettes of cylindrical or flattish, fleshy branches bearing succulent leaves of varying form growing from a central base.

M. guerichianum is a highly succulent annual, with thick, fleshy, cylindrical stems and opposite pairs of oval lower and basal leaves, which are larger than the upper leaves. White or green to yellowish white and pink flowers appear in summer. Propagate from seed in spring, or from cuttings.

Species, variety or cultivar:
–

Other common names:
–

Height and spread:
10 x 45 cm (4 x 18 in)

Blooming period:
Summer

Soil type:
Well-drained, very light, sandy soil

Sun or Shade:
Needs full sun

Hardiness:
Minimum temp –7°C (20°F)

Mimulus • *Monkey Flower*

Description

Roughly 180 species comprise this mostly American genus of upright plants belonging to the foxglove (Scrophulariaceae) family. Stems covered in fine hairs and sticky glands, which may also be present on the leaves, and the flowers, which are short tubes with widely flared throats, form in the leaf axil. Hybrids are strong and vigorous with a wide range of striking colours to choose from, such as 'Highland Pink', which has strong red velvet colours with paler undersides. The flowers are patterned with spots and are said to resemble faces.

In suitably mild climates, the shrubby Mimulus are easy to grow, provided they are given full sun and a well-drained soil that remains moist through summer. They are quick growing, inclined to become untidy unless routinely pinched back. They tend to be short-lived, and can be propagated from seed or half-hardened cuttings. These plants grow along streams and lakes in the wild, and so are suited to bog gardens, or as borders to ponds, as well as for rockeries.

BELOW: *M. angustatus* is one of several Monkey Flower species that grow in wet places. This species, with its distinctive colour pattern, prefers vernal pools, which are natural depressions covered by shallow water for variable periods from winter to spring; they are typically dry for most of summer and autumn.

Species, variety or cultivar:
hybrid cultivar, 'Highland Pink'

Other common names:
Monkey Flower, Musk

Height and spread:
90 x 80 cm (36 x 32 in)

Blooming period:
Summer

Soil type:
Well-drained soil that remains moist through summer

Sun or Shade:
Enjoys full sun to partial shade

Hardiness:
Minimum temp –40°C (–40°F)

Nemesia, hybrid cultivar

Description

Confined to South Africa, this genus in the foxglove (Scrophulariaceae) family includes around 65 species, which form small mounds of toothed linear to lance-shaped foliage. Many hybrids between *N. strumosa* and *N. versicolor*, the modern seedling strains, have been bred to produce early-flowering compact plants in a wide range of colours. They are short-lived, but may be sown in succession from spring through to late summer. 'Innocence' has pure white flowers, each with a small yellow throat. Grow in a sunny position in light free-draining soil kept moist, and pinch back to keep compact. Propagate from seed in late autumn or early spring.

Species, variety or cultivar:
hybrid cultivar, 'Innocence'

Other common names:
–

Height and spread:
40 x 40 cm (16 x 16 in)

Blooming period:
Summer

Soil type:
Light, free-draining soil kept moist

Sun or Shade:
Likes full to part sun

Hardiness:
Minimum temp 4°C (40°F)

Nemesia strumosa

DESCRIPTION

N. strumosa is a popular short-lived bedding plant, native to South Africa, and has bright green, toothed, lower leaves to 8 cm (3 in) long, and upper leaves which are much smaller. The flowers, which have a conspicuous lower lobe, often in a contrasting colour to the upper petals, are borne in clusters on short stems. A fast-growing mounding annual, it produces many small flowers in crowded heads, often in warm shades of yellow-orange and apricot, sometimes purple or white, in summer. Members of the Sachet Series are compact heavy-flowering plants, often fragrant, which come in single colours, such as 'Blueberry Sachet', which is an attractive purple, with a yellow eye.

Species, variety or cultivar:
Sachet Series, 'Blueberry Sachet'

Other common names:
–

Height and spread:
50 x 40 cm (20 x 16 in)

Blooming period:
Summer

Soil type:
Light, free-draining soil kept moist

Sun or Shade:
Likes full to part sun

Hardiness:
Minimum temp –7°C (20°F)

Nemophila maculata • *Five Spot*

Description

There are 11 species of annuals in this genus, which is a member of the waterleaf (Hydrophyllaceae) family. Native to western North America, they have small pinnate leaves on wiry stems, and form spreading mounds of ferny foliage that are smothered in small 5-petalled flowers, usually borne singly in the leaf axils, in late spring and summer. While not spectacular plants, they are graceful and often intriguingly coloured, with flowers in various shades and patterns of blue and white. Although the name, coming from the Greek *nemos* (a glade) and *phileo* (to love), suggests a preference for shade, they are most at home in full sun or half sun.

N. maculata is an annual species from central California, USA. Initially upright, it later spreads, and has soft green pinnate leaves, with up to seven lobes. White flowers, with a purple blotch near the petal tip, are borne in summer.

Species, variety or cultivar:
–

Other common names:
Five Spot

Height and spread:
30 x 50 cm (12 x 20 in)

Blooming period:
Summer

Soil type:
Moist, well-drained soil

Sun or Shade:
Enjoys full sun to half sun

Hardiness:
Minimum temp 4°C (40°F)

LEFT AND ABOVE: This species, also called 'Buffalo Eyes', will tolerate a variety of conditions, and doesn't seem to care whether soil is heavy or sandy. However, it prefers cool weather, so if yours is very hot, try to put this species where it will receive some shade.

Nemophila menziesii

Description

One of 11 species in this genus of annuals, *N. menziesii* is a low spreading example from California, USA, and has ferny light green leaves, with up to 11 lobes. The many white-centred mid-blue flowers, sometimes entirely white, appear in summer. 'Pennie Black' has very dark purple-black flowers, edged with white. These are superb plants for narrow borders, banks, hanging baskets and window boxes, where their semi-trailing habit is shown off to advantage. They require moist, well-drained soil, and propagation is from seed, which is best sown in situ, as once germinated, the young plants resent disturbance.

Species, variety or cultivar:
'Pennie Black'

Other common names:
–

Height and spread:
15 x 50 cm (6 x 20 in)

Blooming period:
Summer

Soil type:
Moist, well-drained soil

Sun or Shade:
Likes full sun to half sun

Hardiness:
Minimum temp 4°C (40°F)

Nicandra physalodes • *Apple of Peru*

Description

This genus of a single species is a member of the nightshade (Solanaceae) family, and is a tall-growing annual native to Peru. The deep green, pointed, oval leaves grow up to 15 cm (6 in) long, with irregularly lobed or toothed edges. Open bell-shaped flowers in purple, blue or mauve, with white centres, are borne in summer and autumn, and only open for a short time each day. They have a reputation for repelling flies, hence the common name, and have a fruit that follows, which is enclosed in a green Chinese lantern-like calyx. Grow in full sun in a rich well-drained soil, and propagate from seed sown in situ after frost danger has passed.

Species, variety or cultivar:
–

Other common names:
Apple of Peru, Shoo Fly

Height and spread:
120 x 60 cm (48 x 24 in)

Blooming period:
Summer and autumn

Soil type:
Rich, well-drained soil

Sun or Shade:
Needs full sun

Hardiness:
Minimum temp –12°C (10°F)

Nicotiana x sanderae • *Tobacco*

Description

Famous as the source of the tobacco leaf, this genus, which is a member of the nightshade (Solanaceae) family, encompasses over 65 species, the bulk of which are annuals and perennials, most native to tropical and subtropical America, with a smaller number in Australia and the South Pacific. Their leaves are very large and covered with fine hairs, sticky to the touch, and may exude a fragrance when crushed. The flowers are tubular or bell-shaped, usually in shades of green, pale yellow, pink or soft red, and if fragrant, their scent is generally released at night.

N. x sanderae is a garden hybrid between *N. alata* and *N. forgetiana,* and is a bushy hairy-leafed annual with slightly crinkled, wavy, dark green, ovate leaves. Fragrant, flaring, tubular flowers, in red, purple and white, open all day. The Saratoga Series is uniform in size, with a mixed colour range of reds, pinks, white and lime.

LEFT: *N. tobaccum*, tobacco. This species has a corolla with a long, narrow tube.

Species, variety or cultivar:
'Saratoga Mixed'

Other common names:
Tobacco

Height and spread:
60 x 25 cm (24 x 10 in)

Blooming period:
Summer

Soil type:
Well-drained and reasonably fertile

Sun or Shade:
Likes full sun to partial shade

Hardiness:
Minimum temp –18°C (0°F)

Nierembergia caerulea • *Cup Flower*

Description

There are about 23 species in this genus, which is native to South America where they grow in moist sunny situations. They are slender stemmed plants, either creeping, spreading or erect, with small narrow leaves. The showy flowers are open and upward-facing, in shades of blue, purple or white, often with yellow throats, and they are borne for long periods from summer to autumn.

N. caerulea is from Argentina and is a small, upright, densely branching perennial often grown as an annual in cooler climates. It has narrow pointed leaves and numerous lavender flowers with yellow throats. 'Purple Robe' has darker purple flowers with yellow throats, which appear in summer.

Species, variety or cultivar:
'Purple Robe'
Other common names:
Cupflower
Height and spread:
20 x 20 cm (8 x 8 in)
Blooming period:
Summer
Soil type:
Gritty moisture-retentive soil
Sun or Shade:
Likes a sunny sheltered position
Hardiness:
Minimum temp –7°C (20°F)

Nigella damascena • *Love-in-a-mist*

Description

N. damascena is a European species with bright green finely cut foliage, somewhat like fennel, and fluffy flowers, in blue, pink or white. Make successive plantings of this species for blooms throughout summer. 'Miss Jekyll' has attractive semi-double sky blue flowers.

These flowers enjoy both full sun or partial shade, and will grow in any well-drained soil. Better results are achieved if they are fertilized once a month with a relatively high phosphorus fertilizer. Dead-head to prolong flowering, and propagate from seed sown directly where it is to grow, since Nigella seedlings resent being transplanted. The plants will reseed.

Species, variety or cultivar:
'Miss Jekyll'

Other common names:
Love-in-a-mist

Height and spread:
50 x 25 cm (20 x 10 in)

Blooming period:
Summer

Soil type:
Any well-drained soil fertilized once a month with a relatively high phosphorus fertilizer

Sun or Shade:
Enjoys both full sun and half sun

Hardiness:
Minimum temp 4°C (40°F)

Nigella sativa • *Black Cumin*

DESCRIPTION

This genus of about 15 species of annuals, from the Mediterranean region and western Asia, is a member of the buttercup (Ranunculaceae) family. All species are easy to grow and feature fine green foliage with bushy growth, and flower colours of sky blue and mixes of white, blue, pink, purple, mauve and rosy red. Nigellas bloom profusely and make good cut flowers. Their decorative seed pods and foliage are also used in dried floral arrangements.

N. sativa is from the Mediterranean and has short, thin, mid-green leaves and delicate white or pale blue flowers, which appear in summer. It is grown for its aromatic seed, which is used as a spice in Middle Eastern cuisine. Mohammed said of it: 'In it is a cure for everything except death.' Grow in full or half sun in any well-drained soil and fertilize once a month with a relatively high phosphorus fertilizer.

LEFT: *N. sativa* is native to the Mediterranean, but has been cultivated in other parts of the world, including North Africa, Saudi Arabia and parts of Asia. The Black Seed of *Nigella* (*below*) has been used by mankind for over 3,000 years, making it one of the safest and longest used herbs in herbal history.

Species, variety or cultivar:
–

Other common names:
Black Cumin, Black Seed, Nutmeg Flower, Roman Coriander

Height and spread:
60 x 30 cm (24 x 12 in)

Blooming period:
Summer

Soil type:
Any well-drained soil fertilized once a month with a relatively high phosphorus fertilizer

Sun or Shade:
Enjoys both full sun and half sun

Hardiness:
Minimum temp –18°C (0°F)

Ocimum basilicum • *Basil*

Description

This genus encompasses 35 species of annuals and perennials from tropical and subtropical Africa and Asia that are known for their aromatic foliage. These herbs belong to the mint (Lamiaceae) family and are generally erect bushy plants, with a distinctive branching habit and narrow oval to elliptic leaves. Their foliage varies from pale to dark green through to dark red and purple. Whorls of tiny tubular flowers appear on short spikes in summer and vary from white to creamy green. O. *basilicum* is from tropical and subtropical Asia, and has oval mid-green leaves, sometimes slightly serrated around the edges, and often hairy on the topside of the leaf.

Species, variety or cultivar:
–

Other common names:
Basil, Sweet Basil

Height and spread:
60 x 30 cm (24 x 12 in)

Blooming period:
Summer

Soil type:
Moist, well-drained soil

Sun or Shade:
Likes a warm sunny position

Hardiness:
Minimum temp –1°C (30°F)

Ocimum basilicum • *Basil*

Description

The foliage of this genus is used to flavour a range of dishes, and these herbs have become favourites with many. Often referred to as the summer herb, Basil was probably first cultivated in India, where it is sacred and is dedicated to the gods Vishnu and Krishna.

O. basilicum is used to flavour many dishes, and has whorls of creamy white flowers, on short spikes, which are borne in summer. The species has a number of cultivars, such as 'Lemon Sweet Danny', which has pointed, pale green, lemon-scented foliage, but which can be temperamental to grow.

Species, variety or cultivar:
'Lemon Sweet Danny'

Other common names:
Basil, Sweet Basil

Height and spread:
60 x 30 cm (24 x 12 in)

Blooming period:
Summer

Soil type:
Moist, well-drained soil

Sun or Shade:
Likes a warm sunny position

Hardiness:
Minimum temp –1°C (30°F)

Ocimum basilicum • *Basil*

Description

This upright, erect, bushy annual species from tropical and subtropical Asia has oval mid-green leaves, sometimes slightly serrated around the edges, and is a popular herb used to flavour a range of dishes. The species can be invasive, so it is best grown in pots, and seed should be disposed of carefully. They need a moist, well-drained soil in a warm sunny position to thrive, do not tolerate frost or cold temperatures, and should be pinched back regularly to encourage bushy growth. There are many cultivars of the species, such as 'Valentino', which is a vigorous compact plant with large leaves and a reputation for being particularly fine-tasting.

Species, variety or cultivar:
'Valentino'

Other common names:
Basil, Sweet Basil

Height and spread:
60 x 30 cm (24 x 12 in)

Blooming period:
Summer

Soil type:
Moist, well-drained soil

Sun or Shade:
Likes a warm sunny position

Hardiness:
Minimum temp –1°C (30°F)

Odontonema callistachyum • *Firespike*

Species, variety or cultivar:
–
Other common names:
Firespike
Height and spread:
1.8 x 0.65 m (72 x 26 in)
Blooming period:
Spring
Soil type:
Rich, well-drained soil
Sun or Shade:
Full sun or bright filtered light
Hardiness:
Minimum temp –1°C (30°F)

Description

One of 25 species in the genus, and native to Central America, this plant has an upright growth habit, with glossy, wavy-edged, oblong leaves tapering to a fine point. Showy inflorescences of waxy-textured, tubular crimson flowers are borne at the branch tips through much of the year. Frost tender, these warm-climate plants need rich soil and regular watering and they like well-drained soil in full sun or bright filtered light in a spot sheltered from wind. The species also makes an excellent container plant for large conservatories. Keep them neat and bushy by pinching out the growing tips.

Osteospermum • *African Daisy*

DESCRIPTION

Mainly from southern Africa, this genus has some 70 species, valued for their carpeting of flowers during the warmer months, year round in milder areas. Mainly low, spreading or mounding plants with simple, broadly toothed, elliptic to spatula-shaped leaves. The flowers are large, with showy rat florets, mainly in pinks and purples or white. Disc florets are an unusual purple-blue that contrasts well with the golden anthers. The name comes from the Greek *osteon*, 'bone' and *sperma*, 'seed', referring to the hard seeds.

Osteospermum species hybridize freely, especially in cultivation, and new forms are constantly being introduced. 'Stardust', which was the first hybrid cultivar promoted in Europe has deep pink flowers and purplish green stems and leaves. An award winner, it is still more popular than many of the newer cultivars, as it is a vigorous and hardy plant, and its flowers remain open for longer during the day.

LEFT AND BELOW: Osteospermums are relatively new to most gardeners, and were almost unheard of 25 years ago. They have risen in popularity in the last decade as they have become more commercially available. Osteospermums have now become very popular as summer bedding plants, either to put in borders or in pots.

Species, variety or cultivar:
hybrid cultivar, 'Stardust'

Other common names:
African Daisy

Height and spread:
30 x 60 cm (12 x 24 in)

Blooming period:
Summer to winter

Soil type:
Light, well-drained soil

Sun or Shade:
Prefers a sunny position

Hardiness:
Minimum temp –7°C (20°F)

Oxalis vulcanicola

DESCRIPTION

This is a huge genus of about 500 species belonging to the wood-sorrel (Oxalidaceae) family. Flower buds are rolled like an umbrella and open to bowl- or cup-shaped 5-petalled blooms, some species only opening in full sunlight. Some of the world's worst weeds belong in Oxalis, but so also do many highly desirable, sometimes difficult-to-keep collector's plants, so careful selection is advised.

O. vulcanicola is a small bushy shrub from Central America with succulent reddish stems, and thick green leaves with three leaflets, sometimes flushed with red. Small bright yellow flowers with fine red veins appear from summer to autumn. Propagation is from seed sown fresh, or from cuttings.

Species, variety or cultivar:
–

Other common names:
–

Height and spread:
50 x 50 cm (20 x 20 in)

Blooming period:
Summer to autumn

Soil type:
Moist soil

Sun or Shade:
Likes sun or part-shade

Hardiness:
Minimum temp –7°C (20°F)

Papaver nudicaule • *Arctic Poppy*

Species, variety or cultivar:
–

Other common names:
Arctic Poppy, Iceland Poppy

Height and spread:
40 x 30 cm (16 x 12 in)

Blooming period:
Spring to summer

Soil type:
Light, moist, well-drained soil

Sun or Shade:
Likes a sunny position

Hardiness:
Minimum temp –46°C (–50°F)

Description

One of about 50 species of annuals and perennials in this readily recognized and widespread group which gives its name to the poppy (Papaveraceae) family, *P. nudicaule* bears solitary long-stemmed flowers to 8 cm (3 in) wide, with four crinkly petals. The flowers appear in many colours, although wild forms are usually white, yellow or orange, and they have a central ovary topped with a prominent stigmatic disc. Very hardy, they prefer a sunny position with light well-drained soil, and can be propagated either by root cuttings or by raising from seed.

Papaver nudicaule • *Arctic Poppy*

DESCRIPTION

This genus of around 50 species of annuals and perennials gives its name to the poppy (Papaveraceae) family. From basal rosettes of usually finely lobed, often hairy leaves emerge bristly upright flower stems, each with one nodding bud, rarely two or three. The flowers most often have four crepe-like petals around a central ovary topped with a prominent stigmatic disc. Today we associate poppies with war remembrance days, though it was Homer, the ninth-century BC Greek poet, who first linked the hanging poppy bud with a dying soldier.

P. nudicaule is a perennial species, often treated as an annual, and is native to subantarctic regions, flowering from spring to summer. It has hairy pinnate leaves, often light blue-green, and bears solitary long-stemmed flowers to 8 cm (3 in) wide, in many colours, although wild forms are usually white, yellow or orange. 'Pacino' has appealing lemon yellow flowers on stocky stems.

LEFT AND BELOW: *P. nudicaule*, the Arctic Poppy, is the best species for cut flowers. Pick just as the buds are beginning to open, and singe the ends before placing them in water.

Species, variety or cultivar:
'Pacino'

Other common names:
Arctic Poppy, Iceland Poppy

Height and spread:
40 x 30 cm (16 x 12 in)

Blooming period:
Spring to summer

Soil type:
Light, moist, well-drained soil

Sun or Shade:
Likes a sunny position

Hardiness:
Minimum temp –46°C (–50°F)

Pelargonium fruticosum • *Storksbill*

Species, variety or cultivar:
–
Other common names:
Storksbill
Height and spread:
40 x 50 cm (16 x 20 in)
Blooming period:
Autumn
Soil type:
Well-drained soil
Sun or Shade:
Enjoys full sun
Hardiness:
Minimum temp –7°C (20°F)

Description

Most of the 250 species of annuals, perennials and subshrubs in this genus of the geranium (Geraniaceae) family come from South Africa, a few from the rest of Africa, Australia and the Middle East. Foliage is variable but often light green, rounded or hand-shaped, with conspicuous lobes, fine hairs and darker blotches, and some have succulent leaves.

P. fruticosum is a low-spreading and mounding spring- to autumn-flowering South African species, with downy bright green leaves divided into short linear segments. The starry, red-stemmed, white to pink flowers sometimes have red basal markings.

Pelargonium, hybrid cultivar • *Storksbill*

DESCRIPTION

Pelargonium species interbreed freely; first hybrids appeared soon after the plants entered cultivation. The parentage of these early crosses is long-lost, but their legacy lives on in a range of hybrid groups of mostly compact plants with large showy flowers.

Dwarf Hybrids resemble Zonal Hybrids in their foliage and stature, but with Regal-like flowers, and are small plants often having fully double blooms, which is their main point of difference from the Angel Hybrids. Flower displays tend to be damaged by rain and so they are best suited for use in pots and window boxes. 'Brackenwood', 20 cm (8 in) tall, has pink double flowers with a white eye.

Species, variety or cultivar:
hybrid cultivar, Dwarf Hybrid, 'Brackenwood'

Other common names:
Storksbill

Height and spread:
20 x 50 cm (8 x 20 in)

Blooming period:
Summer to winter

Soil type:
Light, well-drained soil

Sun or Shade:
Likes full sun

Hardiness:
Minimum temp –7°C (20°F)

Pelargonium, hybrid cultivar • *Storksbill*

Description

There are 250 species within this genus of the geranium (Geraniaceae) family, which comes mainly from South Africa. The flowers are simple 5-petalled structures, often massed and/or brightly coloured, making a spectacular show. The common name comes from the Greek *pelargos*, stork, which refers to the shape of the seed pod. Tolerant of light frost only, many pelargoniums are treated as annuals in areas with cold winters, and are drought tolerant once established.

While the first Pelargonium hybrids appeared soon after the plants entered cultivation, and the parentage of these early crosses is long-lost, their legacy lives on in a range of hybrid groups of mostly compact plants with large showy flowers. Angel Hybrids are similar to Regal Hybrids but are usually only 30 cm (12 in) tall or less and do not produce double flowers. 'Oldbury Duet' has interesting green and white variegated foliage, with upper petals of maroon, and lower petals of light mauve darkening towards the edges.

LEFT AND BELOW: These mostly frost-tender plants grow well in a mild climate and are suitable for both garden beds and pots.

Species, variety or cultivar:
hybrid cultivar, Angel Hybrid, 'Oldbury Duet'

Other common names:
Storksbill

Height and spread:
30 x 50 cm (12 x 20 in)

Blooming period:
Summer to winter

Soil type:
Light, well-drained soil

Sun or Shade:
Likes full sun

Hardiness:
Minimum temp –7°C (20°F)

Pelargonium, hybrid cultivar • *Storksbill*

DESCRIPTION

Among the many Pelargonium hybrid groups are the Regal Hybrids, also known as Martha Washington Hybrids, which are around 50 cm (20 in) tall, though plant sizes can range from dwarfs under 30 cm (12 in) tall through to shrubs of 1.2 m (4 ft) or more. The flowers are large and reminiscent of evergreen azaleas, and they may be single or double, occuring in a huge range of colours and patterns. 'Brown's Butterfly' is a quite stunning example, and is a very dark reddish brown, almost black, lightening to a crimson red on the outer edges of the petals.

Species, variety or cultivar:
hybrid cultivar, Regal Hybrid, 'Brown's Butterfly'

Other common names:
Storksbill

Height and spread:
75 x 100 cm (30 x 40 in)

Blooming period:
Summer to winter

Soil type:
Light, well-drained soil

Sun or Shade:
Likes full sun

Hardiness:
Minimum temp –7°C (20°F)

Pelargonium, hybrid cultivar • *Storksbill*

DESCRIPTION

The 250 species within this genus of the geranium (Geraniaceae) family come mainly from South Africa. Flowers are simple 5-petalled structures, often massed, and brightly coloured. The common name comes from the Greek *pelargos*, stork, referring to the shape of the seed pod. Tolerant of light frost only, many pelargoniums are treated as annuals in areas with cold winters, and are drought tolerant once established.

Unique Hybrids are woody-based plants mostly with *P. fulgidum* parentage, and this shows in their large pinnate leaves. Their foliage is aromatic and the flowers large. 'Bolero' has single flowers, which are vivid pink with a darker centre.

Species, variety or cultivar:
hybrid cultivar, Unique Hybrid, 'Bolero'

Other common names:
Storksbill

Height and spread:
75 x 100 cm (30 x 40 in)

Blooming period:
Summer to winter

Soil type:
Light, well-drained soil

Sun or Shade:
Likes full sun

Hardiness:
Minimum temp –7°C (20°F)

Pelargonium peltatum • *Storksbill*

Description

Most of the 250 species of annuals, perennials and subshrubs in this genus of the geranium (Geraniaceae) family come from South Africa, a few from the rest of Africa, Australia and the Middle East. Foliage is variable but often light green, rounded or hand-shaped, with conspicuous lobes, fine hairs and darker blotches, and some have succulent leaves.

P. peltatum is a sprawling, scrambling, climbing, continuous-flowering, woody-stemmed South African species. Its succulent rounded leaves, with five triangular lobes, are often zonally marked, and the short-stemmed heads consist of up to nine narrow-petalled flowers, which are white or pink in the wild, with darker veined upper petals, appearing from spring to summer.

There are many cultivars in a wide range of flower and foliage colours and forms, such as 'Mini Cascade Red', which has very dark pink to red flowers, darker-veined on the upper petals, which bloom profusely from spring to summer.

LEFT AND BELOW: Pelargoniums make a wonderful display in hanging baskets or in containers.

Species, variety or cultivar:
'Mini Cascade Red'

Other common names:
Storksbill

Height and spread:
75 x 100 cm (30 x 40 in)

Blooming period:
Summer to winter

Soil type:
Light, well-drained soil

Sun or Shade:
Likes full sun

Hardiness:
Minimum temp –7°C (20°F)

Pelargonium, zonal hybrid • *Storksbill*

Description

The Pelargonium Zonal Hybrids, have mainly *P. inquinans x P. zonale* parentage, and many are now classified as *P. x hortorum*. They have a low, bushy habit with succulent stems and light green, rounded to kidney-shaped, shallowly lobed leaves with dark zonal markings, to 10 cm (4 in) wide. Heads of brightly coloured flowers to nearly 2.5 cm (1 in) wide, held clear of the foliage on upright stems, appear throughout the warmer months, year-round in frost-free areas. Among the many cultivars is 'Antik Orange', which has an attractive salmon orange flower and light green leaves, darker green in the centre.

Species, variety or cultivar:
hybrid cultivar, Zonal Hybrid, 'Antik Orange'

Other common names:
Storksbill

Height and spread:
75 x 100 cm (30 x 40 in)

Blooming period:
Summer to winter

Soil type:
Light, well-drained soil

Sun or Shade:
Likes full sun

Hardiness:
Minimum temp –7°C (20°F)

Perilla frutescens • *Beefsteak Plant*

Description

This is a genus of six annual herbs belonging to the mint (Lamiaceae) family, found naturally in Asia from India to Japan. *P. frutescens* is erect, finely hairy, resembles basil, and is native to the Himalayas and eastern Asia. Spikes form, up to 10 cm (4 in) long, of small, white, pink or reddish flowers with a corolla to 4 mm across. The opposite pairs of leaves, which are green or purple, or sometimes speckled with purple, are often wrinkled, and are broadly oval, heavily serrated, pointed and have a scent resembling cinnamon. *P. f. var. crispa* is an attractive plant, with extra-crinkled bronze or dark purplish brown leaves.

Species, variety or cultivar:
var. crispa

Other common names:
Beefsteak Plant, Chinese Basil, Wild Sesame

Height and spread:
100 x 60 cm (40 x 24 in)

Blooming period:
Late summer to autumn

Soil type:
Rich, but well-drained soil

Sun or Shade:
Likes full sun to light shade

Hardiness:
Minimum temp –12°C (10°F)

Petunia x hybrida

Description

Known mainly for the showy annual and perennial hybrids classified as *Petunia x hybrida*, this tropical South American genus from the nightshade (Solanaceae) family includes some 35 species of annuals, perennials and shrubs. Cultivated varieties occur in virtually every colour, but lack the fragrance of some of the species.

P. x hybrida are generally low, spreading, short-living perennials treated as annuals and raised from seed. The Celebrity Series are compact and heavy flowering, and have several colour mixes, such as 'Celebrity Blue Ice', which has light mauve petals, darkening toward a veined centre.

Species, variety or cultivar:
Celebrity Series, 'Celebrity Ice Blue'

Other common names:
–

Height and spread:
40 x 100 cm (16 x 40 in)

Blooming period:
Summer

Soil type:
Moist, humus-rich, well-drained soil

Sun or Shade:
Enjoys full sun to part shade

Hardiness:
Minimum temp –7°C (20°F)

Petunia x hybrida

Species, variety or cultivar:
Wave Series, 'Purple Wave'

Other common names:
–

Height and spread:
40 x 100 cm (16 x 40 in)

Blooming period:
Summer

Soil type:
Moist, humus-rich, well-drained soil

Sun or Shade:
Enjoys full sun to part shade

Hardiness:
Minimum temp –7°C (20°F)

Description

This tropical South American genus from the nightshade (Solanaceae) family includes some 35 species of annuals, perennials and shrubs, and is known mainly for the showy annual and perennial hybrids classified as *Petunia x hybrida*. These garden hybrids are mainly crosses between *P. axillaris* and *P. integrifolia*, and are usually low, spreading, short-lived perennials treated as annuals and grown from seed.

The Wave Series is characterized by mounding bushes and large flowers. 'Purple Wave' is an incredibly fast-growing member of this group with abundant pink-purple flowers that are borne for much of the year. Dead-heading is not necessary, but its habit to quickly spread means that it may be more suited to a large pot in some situations.

Petunia x hybrida

Description

Known mainly for the showy annual and perennial hybrids classified as *Petunia x hybrida*, this tropical South American genus from the nightshade (Solanaceae) family includes some 35 species of annuals, perennials and shrubs. The genus is closely allied to tobacco (Nicotiana), and its name is derived from the Tupian Indian word *petun*, 'tobacco'. Most are low-spreading plants with soft, downy, rounded leaves and large funnel-shaped flowers with five fused lobes. Although lacking the fragrance of some of the species, cultivated varieties occur in virtually every colour.

Garden hybrids, mostly between *P. axillaris* and *P. integrifolia*, comprise *P. x hybrida*, and are usually low, spreading, short-lived perennials raised from seed and treated as annuals. The Mirage Series is characterized by large single flowers, often in light colours, with striking contrasting dark veins, such as the distinctive scarlet-flowered 'Mirage Red'.

Species, variety or cultivar:
Mirage Series, 'Mirage Red'

Other common names:
–

Height and spread:
40 x 100 cm (16 x 40 in)

Blooming period:
Summer

Soil type:
Moist, humus-rich, well-drained soil

Sun or Shade:
Enjoys full sun to part shade

Hardiness:
Minimum temp –7°C (20°F)

Phacelia campanularia • *California Bluebell*

Description

This genus of about 150 glandular, hairy, annual, biennial or perennial herbs is a member of the waterleaf (Hydrophyllaceae) family, and originates from North and South America. The genus name comes from the Greek *phakelos* (cluster) – a reference to the dense white to purple flowerheads.

P. campanularia is an annual herb from sandy or gravelly dry or desert regions of southern California, USA. Elliptical to oval, toothed leaves grow on simple, short-haired, erect stems, and loose clusters of dark blue bell-shaped flowers to 3.5 cm (1½ in) across, spotted with white, appear in early spring.

Species, variety or cultivar:
–

Other common names:
California Bluebell, Desert Bluebell, Wild Canterbury Bell

Height and spread:
60 x 60 cm (24 x 24 in)

Blooming period:
Spring

Soil type:
Fertile, well-drained soil

Sun or Shade:
Likes full sun

Hardiness:
Minimum temp –18°C (0°F)

Phacelia tanacetifolia • *Fiddleneck*

Description

The plants in this genus of around 150 species of hairy, glandular species grow from thick tap roots, have alternate leaves, divided or smooth-edged, and bear dense terminal heads of white to purple flowers, which have a narrow 5-lobed calyx and an open to spreading bell-shaped corolla with lobed petals.

P. tanacetifolia is a moderately fast-growing annual from California, USA to Mexico, is covered with bristly hairs, and has an erect, sparsely branched stem and compound, oval to oblong, toothed or lobed leaves. The flowers have a wide, bell-shaped corolla coloured blue, lilac or mauve, and appear in spring.

Species, variety or cultivar:
–
Other common names:
Fiddleneck
Height and spread:
150 x 60 cm
(60 x 20 in)
Blooming period:
Spring
Soil type:
Fertile, well-drained soil
Sun or Shade:
Likes full sun
Hardiness:
Minimum temp –18°C
(0°F)

Phlox drummondii

Description

This North American genus of 67 annuals and perennials belongs in the phlox (Polemoniaceae) family. All types have similar terminal heads of small bell-shaped flowers with long widely flaring tubes, but growth habits differ markedly. Phlox is Greek for 'flame' – a very appropriate epithet for the annual, rock and border types, with their vivid bursts of incandescent colour.

P. drummondii, a native to Texas, USA, is now widely established as a wildflower, and has upright, sometimes sprawling stems with pointed oval to narrow lance-shaped leaves. Showy heads of small flowers, bright lavender to purple-red, often with notched petals, appear in summer.

Species, variety or cultivar:
–

Other common names:
–

Height and spread:
40 x 40 cm (16 x 16 in)

Blooming period:
Summer

Soil type:
Well-drained soil that can be kept moist

Sun or Shade:
Needs full sun

Hardiness:
Minimum temp –23°C (–10°F)

Plumbago auriculata • *Cape Leadwort*

Description

There are about 15 species of annuals, perennials and shrubs in this genus, widely distributed throughout the tropics and subtropics. They have simple light to mid-green leaves and can become rather sparsely foliaged and twiggy if not trimmed. Their main attraction is their flowers, which appear throughout the warmer months. Carried on short racemes, they are very narrow tubes tipped with five relatively large lobes, and come in white or various shades of pink and blue.

P. auriculata is from South Africa and is a tough, vigorous shrub with long arching stems. Profuse pale blue flowers are borne throughout the warmer months.

Species, variety or cultivar:
–

Other common names:
Cape Leadwort, Plumbago

Height and spread:
4.5 x 2 m (15 x 7 ft)

Blooming period:
Throughout the warmer months

Soil type:
Moist, well-drained soil

Sun or Shade:
Likes full sun

Hardiness:
Minimum temp –7°C (20°F)

Portulaca grandiflora • *Moss Rose*

Description

This genus of some 40 species occurring in the warmer parts of the world belongs to the purslane (Portulacaceae) family, and are mostly succulent herbs, usually with tuberous roots. The leaves are flat or cylindrical, opposite or spirally arranged, usually with hairs in their axils, and the flowers are solitary or in heads, surrounded by a whorl of bracts formed by the upper leaves. There are two sepals and usually five pink, purple or yellow petals which open in direct sun and close in shade.

P. grandiflora is a slow-growing annual, native to Brazil, Argentina and Uruguay, and has a partially prostrate or climbing stem, to 30 cm (12 in) long, with reddish twigs and alternate, thick, fleshy, lance-shaped, cylindrical, pale green leaves. Single or double flowers of rose, red, purple, lavender, yellow or white, often striped, open only in sunlight. 'Double Mix' is a popular cultivar and has rose-shaped flowers in various bright colours.

Species, variety or cultivar:
'Double Mix'

Other common names:
Eleven-O'clock, Garden Portaluca, Moss Rose, Rose Moss, Sun Plant

Height and spread:
30 x 30 cm (12 x 12 in)

Blooming period:
Spring to autumn

Soil type:
Well-drained soils

Sun or Shade:
Enjoys a sunny sheltered position

Hardiness:
Minimum temp –12°C (10°F)

FAR LEFT AND LEFT:
Moss Rose is a nice ground cover for dry areas, borders and beds in the sun. It also makes a good hanging basket plant. The 2.5 cm (1 in) wide flowers close in the afternoon to reopen in the morning.

Portulaca grandiflora • *Moss Rose*

DESCRIPTION

With around 40 species occurring in the warmer parts of the world, this genus of mostly succulent herbs, usually with tuberous roots, belongs to the purslane (Portulacaceae) family. The flowers are solitary or in heads, surrounded by a whorl of bracts formed by the upper leaves, the Australian Species with distinct stalks. The fruit is a small conical capsule, opening when the top falls off to release the many small seeds. Some are grown as ornamentals, some for eating.

P. grandiflora, native to Brazil, Argentina and Uruguay, has a partially prostrate or climbing stem, to 30 cm (12 in) long. It is a slow-growing annual, with reddish twigs and alternate, thick, fleshy, lance-shaped, cylindrical, pale green leaves. Single or double flowers of rose, red, purple, lavender, yellow or white, often striped, open only in sunlight. Among the popular cultivars is the Sundial Series, and 'Sundial Gold', as the name would suggest, has attractive golden yellow blooms.

BELOW AND RIGHT: 'Double' moss roses produce flowers ranging from 2.5–5 cm (1–2 in) in many of the brightest possible colours, and some of them really do look like rose blossoms though set amidst succulent leaves instead of amidst thorny rose stems.

Species, variety or cultivar:
'Sundial Gold'
Other common names:
Eleven-O'clock, Garden Portaluca, Moss Rose, Rose Moss, Sun Plant
Height and spread:
30 x 30 cm (12 x 12 in)
Blooming period:
Spring to autumn
Soil type:
Well-drained soils
Sun or Shade:
Enjoys a sunny sheltered position
Hardiness:
Minimum temp –12°C (10°F)

Ratbida columnifera • *Prairie Coneflower*

Description

Commonly known as the prairie coneflower, this genus in the daisy (Asteraceae) family contains five species that are widespread throughout North America, from Ontario, Canada, through to New York, Minnesota, South Dakota, Nebraska and south to Georgia and Texas. These plants are stiff and erect, with deeply cut leaves covered with rigid hairs. The crushed seed heads have an aromatic anise scent. The genus was named by wanderer-botanist Constantine Rafinesque-Schmaltz (1773–1840), who often assigned unexplained names to plants.

R. columnifera is found from North America to Mexico, and has hairy grey-green leaves. Flowers that are bright yellow or brown-purple, are borne in drooping rays, in summer–autumn, and the floral disc is cylindrical or columnar, and brown.

Species, variety or cultivar:
–

Other common names:
Long-head Coneflower, Mexican Hat, Prairie Coneflower

Height and spread:
60 x 45 cm (24 x 18 in)

Blooming period:
Summer to autumn

Soil type:
Well-drained soil

Sun or Shade:
Prefers full sun

Hardiness:
Minimum temp –34°C (–30°F)

Reseda lutea • *Yellow Mignonette*

Description

A genus of some 50 to 60 species of annuals and perennials giving its name to the mignonette (Resedaceae) family, occurring mainly in the Mediterranean area, with some species coming from India, Asia and East Africa.

R. lutea is an annual herb found from the Mediterranean to Iran, which has deep roots and many erect, very fast-growing stems. The leaves are simple blades or have one to three deep lobes, with or without stalks, and the flowers, which have four to eight white-edged sepals, and four to eight yellow petals, each with two to three lobes, appear in summer. The fruit is an erect three-parted capsule containing smooth seed.

Species, variety or cultivar:
–
Other common names:
Yellow Mignonette
Height and spread:
70 x 70 cm (27 x 27 in)
Blooming period:
Summer
Soil type:
Fertile, well-drained, preferably alkaline soil
Sun or Shade:
Likes a sunny site
Hardiness:
Minimum temp –18°C (0°F)

Reseda odorata • *Mignonette*

DESCRIPTION

The 50 to 60 species in this genus have small leaves that can be smooth-edged or lobed to toothed, and bear tiny flowers in upright spikes that are rarely showy, usually green or white, and in some species sweetly fragrant. All grow well in a sunny site in fertile, well-drained, and preferably alkaline soils.

R. odorata is a well-known annual from the Mediterranean region, with smooth-edged leaves, occasionally 3-lobed. Loose clusters of highly scented, tiny, greenish white flowers, with tufts of soft orange stamens, are borne in early summer, and the species is cultivated for an essential oil used in the perfume industry. Makes a good bee-attracting plant.

Species, variety or cultivar:
–

Other common names:
Bastard Rocket, Mignonette, Sweet Reseda

Height and spread:
60 x 20 cm (24 x 8 in)

Blooming period:
Summer

Soil type:
Fertile, well-drained, preferably alkaline soil

Sun or Shade:
Enjoys a sunny site

Hardiness:
Minimum temp –23°C (–10°F)

Rhodanthe manglesii • *Swan River Everlasting*

DESCRIPTION

This genus in the daisy (Asteraceae) family, one of several in the complex Helichrysum group, was extensively revised in the early 1990s and is now considered to be exclusively Australian. The 40 species in the genus are annuals, perennials and small shrubs with simple, narrow, light green to silver-grey leaves. They are rather sprawling plants grown for their long-lasting show of flowers, which are made colourful by dry, papery, petal-like structures known as phyllaries.

R. manglesii is a Western Australian annual and has erect stems with pointed oval to narrow heart-shaped, grey-green to blue-green leaves, to 5 cm (2 in) long. Many white to light pink flowerheads, 3 cm (1¼ in) wide, bloom in spring or after rain.

Species, variety or cultivar:
–

Other common names:
Swan River Everlasting

Height and spread:
45 x 30 cm (18 x 12 in)

Blooming period:
Spring

Soil type:
Light, gritty, very free-draining soil

Sun or Shade:
Enjoys full sun

Hardiness:
Minimum temp –12°C (10°F)

Ricinus communis • *Caster Oil Plant*

Description

A member of the spurge (Euphorbiaceae) family, this fast-growing single-species genus from northeast Africa has naturalized throughout the tropical regions where it can grow to 12 m (40 ft) high in the wild. It is considered a prized annual in many cold-climate gardens, where it is grown for its deeply lobed, and often coloured, leaves.

Ricinus requires fertile soil with ample organic matter added to ensure moisture retention and free drainage. Although a full sun position suits this plant, its brittle stems need to be protected from winds and frost. When grown from seed care must be taken as the seed coats, and other parts of the plant, are extremely toxic.

Species, variety or cultivar:
–

Other common names:
Castor Bean Plant, Castor Oil Plant

Height and spread:
1.5 x 0.9 m (5 x 3 ft)

Blooming period:
–

Soil type:
Fertile, moisture-retentive soil with free drainage

Sun or Shade:
Prefers full sun

Hardiness:
Minimum temp –7°C (20°F)

Rudbeckia hirta • *Black-eyed Susan*

Description

This North American genus of 15 species of perennials, belonging to the daisy (Asteraceae) family, is very popular in gardens because of the plants' great hardiness, ease of cultivation and valuable late-season flower display. Most are fairly bulky plants, over 1.2 m (4 ft) tall, and from late summer they carry masses of large golden yellow daisies, usually with dark brown to black disc florets.

R. hirta is a biennial or short-lived perennial, native to central USA, whose dwarf forms are often treated as annuals. Narrow, 10 cm (4 in) long, lance-shaped leaves are toothed, with flowerheads to nearly 10 cm (4 in) wide, with yellow ray florets, and purple-brown disc florets, appear in summer–autumn.

Species, variety or cultivar:
–

Other common names:
Black-eyed Susan, Coneflower

Height and spread:
2 x 0.12 m (7 x 4 ft)

Blooming period:
Summer to autumn

Soil type:
Moist, well-drained soil

Sun or Shade:
Sun or shade

Hardiness:
Minimum temp –34°C (–30°F)

Salvia coccinea • *Texas Sage*

Description

This genus, the largest in the mint (Lamiaceae) family, contains about 900 species of annuals, perennials and softwooded evergreen shrubs and grows in a wide range of habitats, from coastal to alpine. Over half the species are native to the Americas. The leaves are always opposite and carried on squared hairy stems, and are aromatic when crushed.

S. coccinea is an annual or short-lived shrub from tropical South America, which in mild climates may be perennial, but elsewhere is treated as an annual. Its hairy, green leaves are mostly triangular, with scalloped margins. The flowers are usually scarlet but may be red, pink, salmon or white.

Species, variety or cultivar:
–

Other common names:
Texas Sage, Tropical Sage

Height and spread:
100 x 80 cm (40 x 32 in)

Blooming period:
Summer to autumn

Soil type:
Well-drained soil

Sun or Shade:
Likes full sun

Hardiness:
Minimum temp –7°C (20°F)

Salvia splendens • *Scarlet Sage*

Species, variety or cultivar:
'Empire Purple'

Other common names:
Black-eyed Susan, Coneflower

Height and spread:
120 x 80 cm (48 x 32 in)

Blooming period:
Spring to summer

Soil type:
Well-drained soil

Sun or Shade:
Sun or shade

Hardiness:
Minimum temp –7°C (20°F)

Description

This genus is the largest in the mint (Lamiaceae) family, and contains about 900 species of annuals, perennials and softwooded evergreen shrubs. The flowers are tubular with the petals split into two lips, which may be straight or flaring, and the colour range extends through shades of blue to purple, and pink to red, as well as white and some yellows.

S. splendens is a variable perennial species, native to Brazil, which is often treated as an annual. It is a much-branched plant, with oval green leaves, serrated along the margins. The flowers are usually red, but there are many other coloured cultivars, such as 'Empire Purple', which has deep reddish purple flowers.

Salvia splendens • *Scarlet Sage*

DESCRIPTION

This genus, the largest in the mint (Lamiaceae) family, contains about 900 species of annuals, perennials and softwooded evergreen shrubs. It grows in a wide range of habitats, from coastal to alpine, with over half the species native to the Americas. The leaves are always opposite and carried on squared hairy stems, and are aromatic when crushed. The flowers are tubular with the petals split into two lips, which may be straight or flaring. The colour range extends through shades of blue to purple, and pink to red, as well as white and some yellows.

The Brazilian species *S. splendens* is a variable perennial, often treated as an annual, and is a much-branched plant with oval green leaves that have serrated margins. Although the flowers are usually red, there are many other coloured cultivars, such as 'Vista Salmon', which is a compact and well-branched plant, with dark green leaves and salmon flowers, with pink inner petals, which are borne on well-packed spikes.

Species, variety or cultivar:
'Vista Salmon'
Other common names:
Scarlet Sage
Height and spread:
120 x 80 cm (48 x 32 in)
Blooming period:
Spring to summer
Soil type:
Well-drained soil
Sun or Shade:
Sun or shade
Hardiness:
Minimum temp –7°C (20°F)

Salvia uliginosa • *Bog Sage*

Description

This species from Brazil, Uruguay and Argentina, is just one of about 900 species in the genus, and is a clump-forming plant, spreading by underground runners. Yellowish green lance-shaped leaves are borne on erect stems, and small sky blue and white flowers, growing in whorls, appear in late summer through to autumn.

S. uliginosa, like most salvias, dislikes heavy wet soils and is best grown in full sun in a well-drained situation. Prune in spring to remove straggly, bare and frost-damaged stems, and propagate from softwood cuttings taken throughout the growing season, or by seed, which can be sown in spring.

Species, variety or cultivar:
–
Other common names:
Bog Sage
Height and spread:
1.8 x 0.9 m (6 x 3 ft)
Blooming period:
Summer to autumn
Soil type:
Well-drained soil
Sun or Shade:
Sun or shade
Hardiness:
Minimum temp –23°C (–10°F)

Sanvitalia procumbens • *Creeping Zinnia*

Species, variety or cultivar:
'Aztec Gold'

Other common names:
Creeping Zinnia

Height and spread:
20 x 30 cm (8 x 12 in)

Blooming period:
Summer

Soil type:
Well-drained good soil

Sun or Shade:
Likes an open sunny position

Hardiness:
Minimum temp –23°C (–10°F)

Description

This genus, comprising seven species found in Mexico and Central America, belongs to the daisy (Asteraceae) family. They are small ornamental shrubs or low-growing perennials, or annuals and have opposite leaves, with sheathing bases, which may be smooth-edged or lobed. The flowers have a daisy-like appearance, the outer florets having rays that are orange to yellow to white, and the disc florets being of various colours, usually a deep purple.

S. procumbens is a low, spreading annual from southwestern USA and Mexico, which forms mats of hairy mid-green leaves, smothered with bright yellow to orange daisies, with purple-black centres, in summer. 'Aztec Gold' is a cultivar with bright yellow, green centred daisies.

Scabiosa atropurpurea • *Egyptian Rose*

Description

A member of the teasel (Dipsacaceae) family, this genus comprises around 80 species of annuals and perennials found from Europe and North Africa to Japan. Most species form a spreading basal clump of light green to grey-green, rounded to lance-shaped leaves with deeply incised notches or lobes. The flowers are individually tiny but occur in rounded to flattened composite heads on stems held clear of the foliage. White and pale yellow to soft pink, or powder blue and mauve are the usual colours.

S. atropurpurea is an annual, biennial or short-lived perennial from South Africa that has a basal cluster of light green to grey-green, lobed or toothed leaves to 15 cm (6 in) long, and shorter upper leaves, which are more deeply lobed, almost pinnate. The fragrant flowerheads are crimson to deep purple-black, grow to 5 cm (2 in) wide, and appear in summer–early autumn. 'Chile Black' is 60 cm (24 in) tall, and has deep black-red flowers with minute lavender flecks.

LEFT AND BELOW: The colour of this flower is a rich, velvety, dark, dark crimson with white 'pins' forming the large 'pincushion' blooms. This strain is grown mainly for cut flower use with blooms that last up to two weeks in a vase.

Species, variety or cultivar:
'Chile Black'

Other common names:
Egyptian Rose, Mournful Widow, Sweet Scabious

Height and spread:
90 x 75 cm (36 x 30 in)

Blooming period:
Summer to autumn

Soil type:
Fertile, moist, free-draining, slightly alkaline soil

Sun or Shade:
Enjoys full sun

Hardiness:
Minimum temp –12°C (10°F)

Scabiosa atropurpurea • *Egyptian Rose*

Species, variety or cultivar:
'Peter Ray'
Other common names:
Egyptian Rose, Mournful Widow, Sweet Scabious
Height and spread:
90 x 75 cm (36 x 30 in)
Blooming period:
Summer to autumn
Soil type:
Fertile, moist, free-draining, slightly alkaline soil
Sun or Shade:
Enjoys full sun
Hardiness:
Minimum temp –12°C (10°F)

Description

An unpleasant sounding name, Scabiosa is derived from scabies, a Latin word for scurf or mange, which was said to be relieved by rubbing with the leaves of these plants. Most species form a spreading basal clump of light green to grey-green, rounded to lance-shaped leaves with deeply incised notches or lobes, and *S. atropurpurea* is no exception, with basal leaves to 15 cm (6 in) long. This South African annual has crimson to deep purple-black, fragrant flowers, to 5 cm (2 in) wide, which are borne from summer to early autumn. 'Peter Ray' grows to 60 cm (24 in) tall, and has attractive large purple-black flowerheads.

Schizanthus • *Poor Man's Orchid*

Description

This Chilean genus of 12 species of annuals and biennials is in the nightshade (Solanaceae) family, though that relationship is well hidden. The cultivated species are small upright plants around 30 cm (12 in) tall, with soft green ferny foliage, often covered with fine hairs. Flowers are borne in branching panicles held above the foliage and are beautifully marked and shaped, with a prominent lower lip, hence the name Poor Man's Orchid.

S. x wisetonensis is a garden hybrid annual of *S. pinnatus x S. grahamii* parentage. Several cultivars resembling *S. pinnatus* in foliage and habit. Flowers in various colours, including white, pink to purple-brown and blue.

Species, variety or cultivar:
x wisetonensis

Other common names:
Poor Man's Orchid

Height and spread:
50 x 30 cm (20 x 12 in)

Blooming period:
Spring to summer

Soil type:
Fertile, moist, well-drained soil

Sun or Shade:
Enjoys full sun or part sun

Hardiness:
Minimum temp –7°C (20°F)

Senecio cineraria • *Dusty Miller*

DESCRIPTION

There are 1,250 species in this cosmopolitan genus of trees, shrubs, lianas, annuals, biennials and perennials within the daisy (Asteraceae) family, making it one of the largest genera of flowering plants. The leaves are lobed or smooth-edged, and the daisy-like flowers are usually arranged in corymbs. Appearing with or without florets, the flowers are usually yellow but can be purple, white, red or blue. Many senecios are toxic to livestock. With such a large genus, cultivation requirements are diverse, so general guidelines only can be given. Plants that are grown in pots in colder climates will need fertile, well-drained soil with added grit and leaf mould. They should be fed and watered moderately during the growing season. Propagation is from seed or cuttings.

S. cineraria is a mounding subshrub originally from southern Europe, but now also naturalized in southern England. The intensely silver-white leaves are deeply dissected and lobed, and small heads of yellow daisy flowers are borne in summer. 'Cirrus' is a cultivar with grey-blue, rounded-lobed leaves.

LEFT AND ABOVE: A very pretty foliage plant in its own right, *Cineraria* 'Cirrus' will also act as a foil to more colourful bedding plants. The silvery broad, felty leaves add a touch of elegance in beds or containers all through the summer and autumn. Very easy to raise from seed.

Species, variety or cultivar:
'Cirrus'

Other common names:
Dusty Miller, Sea Ragwort

Height and spread:
50 x 40 cm (20 x 16 in)

Blooming period:
Summer

Soil type:
Moderately fertile, well-drained soil

Sun or Shade:
Enjoys full sun

Hardiness:
Minimum temp –7°C (20°F)

Silybum marianum • *Blessed Thistle*

Species, variety or cultivar:
–

Other common names:
Blessed Thistle, Our Lady's Milk Thistle

Height and spread:
1.2 x 0.6 m (4 x 2 ft)

Blooming period:
Spring and summer

Soil type:
Free-draining soil

Sun or Shade:
Needs full sun

Hardiness:
Minimum temp –23°C (–10°F)

Description

This genus in the daisy family (Asteraceae) contains just two species, grown for their ornamental foliage. They are native to the Mediterranean region, Europe and eastern Africa where they grow in sunny free-draining areas. The purple thistle flowers are borne on tall stems in spring or summer.

S. marianum, native to Europe, and now naturalized in the Americas, is a robust upright plant that has a basal rosette of long, deeply lobed, dark green leaves with prominent white veins and spiny margins. Purplish thistle flowers are borne in spring and summer. This species has long been used to stimulate milk supply in nursing mothers.

Sutera cordata

Species, variety or cultivar:
–
Other common names:
–
Height and spread:
8 x 50 cm (3 x 20 in)
Blooming period:
Most of the year
Soil type:
Free-draining fertile soil
Sun or Shade:
Likes full sun
Hardiness:
Minimum temp –7°C (20°F)

Description

There are about 130 species of perennials and annuals in this genus from the figwort or foxglove (Scrophulariaceae) family, which originates from South Africa. Small, rounded, toothed, green leaves sit on thin stems that hug the ground. Starry white, mauve, lilac, pink or blue flowers sit face-up on the foliage and the plants can flower for up to ten months of the year.

S. cordata is a low-growing, ground covering plant with pale green leaves borne throughout the year. Pure white flowers with a delicate yellow eye appear almost year round in warmer climates. 'Snowflake' bears tiny white flowers in leaf axils.

Sutera, hybrid cultivar

DESCRIPTION

The roughly 130 species of perennials and annuals in this genus from South Africa, have become well known in recent years as hanging basket plants, and breeders all over the world have been working to produce new colours of these reliable plants, which can flower for up to ten months of the year. Small, rounded, toothed, green leaves sit on thin ground-hugging stems, and starry white, mauve, lilac, pink or blue flowers sit face-up on the foliage and the plants.

Sutera species need free-draining fertile soil to thrive, and are adaptable to sun and shade. During the warmer months they need extra water to keep blooming. Propagate from stem cuttings in autumn or by sowing seed in spring. The many creeping hybrid cultivars that have been developed are ideal for hanging baskets, with dull green foliage and blooms of various colours. 'Snow Storm' has a more compact plant habit, and attractive large pure white flowers.

LEFT AND BELOW: Low spreading compact foliage makes this variety a terrific ground cover or mixed planting in a tub or basket. Each flower is displayed on an upright peduncle which raises the blossom slightly above the foliage. The additive effect of hundreds of delicate flowers creates a brilliant white 'blanket of snow'.

Species, variety or cultivar:
'Snow Storm'
Other common names:
–
Height and spread:
10 x 70 cm (4 x 27 in)
Blooming period:
All year
Soil type:
Free-draining fertile soil
Sun or Shade:
Enjoys full sun
Hardiness:
Minimum temp –7°C (20°F)

Tagetes, hybrid cultivar • *Marigold*

Species, variety or cultivar:
Antigua Series, 'Antigua Gold'
Other common names:
Marigold
Height and spread:
30 x 30 cm (12 x 12 in)
Blooming period:
Summer
Soil type:
Light, well-drained soil
Sun or Shade:
Prefers a warm sunny position
Hardiness:
Minimum temp 4°C (40°F)

Description

All but one of the 50-odd species of this genus in the daisy (Asteraceae) family originates in the American tropics and subtropics. Their flowers, usually yellow or orange, are often daisy-like, with obvious ray and disc florets, although in some forms the disc florets are largely hidden.

Hybrid cultivars are mainly derived from the French marigold (*T. patula*), and these border marigolds are popular for summer bedding. They are usually marketed as seedling series, in mixed or individual colours, and are mostly double flowers with few visible ray florets, predominantly in yellow, orange and red shades. The Antigua Series has flowerheads to 8 cm (3 in) wide, such as 'Antigua Gold', which is a rich golden yellow.

Tagetes, hybrid cultivar • *Marigold*

Species, variety or cultivar:
Atlantis Series, 'Atlantis Primrose'

Other common names:
Marigold

Height and spread:
30 x 30 cm (12 x 12 in)

Blooming period:
Summer

Soil type:
Light, well-drained soil

Sun or Shade:
Prefers a warm sunny position

Hardiness:
Minimum temp 4°C (40°F)

Description

This genus in the daisy (Asteraceae) family has around 50 species, which almost all originate in the American tropics and subtropics. Hybrid cultivars are mainly derived from the French marigold (*T. patula*), and these border marigolds are popular for summer bedding. They are usually marketed as seedling series, in mixed or individual colours, and are mostly double flowers with few visible ray florets, predominantly in yellow, orange and red shades. The Atlantis Series is characterized by pompon-like flowerheads up to 10 cm (4 in) wide, and 'Atlantis Primrose' is a good example, with bright lemon yellow blooms.

Tagetes, hybrid cultivar • *Marigold*

DESCRIPTION

All but one of the 50-odd species of this genus in the daisy (Asteraceae) family originates in the American tropics and subtropics, and they are mainly upright annuals or perennials with dark green, sometimes aromatic, pinnate leaves with toothed edges. Their flowers, usually yellow or orange, are often daisy-like, with obvious ray and disc florets, although in some forms the disc florets are largely hidden.

The majority of hybrid cultivars are derived from the French marigold (*T. patula*), and these border marigolds are popular for summer bedding. They are usually marketed as seedling series, in mixed or individual colours, and are mostly double flowers with few visible ray florets, predominantly in yellow, orange and red shades. The Bonanza Series is recognizable by its crested flowerheads to 5 cm (2 in) wide, such as 'Bonanza Bolero', which has orange blooms, darkening to a red-orange at the petal tips.

LEFT AND BELOW: The Bonanza Series of *Tagetes patula* includes robust plants producing dense flowerheads in yellow and orange tones, as shown by 'Bonanza Bolero'.

Species, variety or cultivar:
Bonanza Series, 'Bonanza Bolero'

Other common names:
Marigold

Height and spread:
30 x 30 cm (12 x 12 in)

Blooming period:
Summer

Soil type:
Light, well-drained soil

Sun or Shade:
Prefers a warm sunny position

Hardiness:
Minimum temp 4°C (40°F)

Tagetes, hybrid cultivar • *Marigold*

Species, variety or cultivar:
'Jolly Jester'
Other common names:
Marigold
Height and spread:
30 x 30 cm (12 x 12 in)
Blooming period:
Summer
Soil type:
Light, well-drained soil
Sun or Shade:
Prefers a warm sunny position
Hardiness:
Minimum temp 4°C (40°F)

DESCRIPTION

Tagetes species almost all originate from the American tropics and subtropics. The genus name, referring to the marigold's habit of just popping up from seed, comes from Tages, an Etruscan deity, and grandson of Jupiter, who sprang from the plowed earth.

Primarily derived from the French marigold (*T. patula*), hybrid cultivar marigolds are popular for summer bedding, and are usually marketed as seedling series, in mixed or individual colours. They have mostly double flowers with few visible ray florets, predominantly in yellow, orange and red shades. 'Jolly Jester' is an incredibly striking cultivar, with its petals distinctively striped in bright yellow and maroon.

Tagetes, hybrid cultivar • *Marigold*

Species, variety or cultivar:
Little Hero Series, 'Little Hero Fire'

Other common names:
Marigold

Height and spread:
12 x 12 in. (30 x 30 cm)

Blooming period:
Summer

Soil type:
Light, well-drained soil

Sun or Shade:
Prefers a warm sunny position

Hardiness:
Minimum temp 40°F (4°C)

Description

Species belonging to this genus in the daisy (Asteraceae) family are mainly upright annuals or perennials with dark green, sometimes aromatic, pinnate leaves with toothed edges, and flowers, which are usually yellow or orange, and often daisy-like, with obvious ray and disc florets.

There are many hybrid cultivars, usually marketed as seedling series, in mixed or individual colours, and which are mostly double flowers with few visible ray florets, predominantly in yellow, orange, and red shades. Little Hero Series is typified by double flowerheads to 5 cm (2 in) wide, such as 'Little Hero Fire', which has a yellow flower with contrasting red inner petals.

Tagetes, hybrid cultivar • *Marigold*

DESCRIPTION

The genus name Tagetes, comes from *Tages*, an Etruscan deity, and grandson of Jupiter, who sprang from the ploughed earth, and it refers to the marigold's habit of just popping up from seed. Marigolds prefer a warm sunny position in light, well-drained soil. Water well and feed if the foliage begins to yellow. Dead-head frequently to ensure continuous blooming. Propagate from seed, which is usually started indoors in early spring.

The many hybrid cultivars are primarily derived from the French marigold (*T. patula*), and are very popular for summer bedding. They are usually marketed as seedlıng series, in mixed or individual colours, and are mostly double flowers with few visible ray florets, predominantly in yellow, orange and red shades. The Safari Series is characterized by double flowers to 8 cm (3 in) wide, such as those seen on 'Safari Red', which has rich red petals outlined by bright yellow borders.

BELOW: 'Safari Yellow' bears heads of broad-petalled bright yellow flowers that are suitable in a mixed border or in a sunny window box. The Safari Series is a long lasting and easy to grow variety that is quick to bloom and will produce large, very double flowers in a good range of colours (many of which have won international awards). A good performer both in the garden and in patio containers.

Species, variety or cultivar:
Safari Series, 'Safari Red'
Other common names:
Marigold
Height and spread:
30 x 30 cm (12 x 12 in)
Blooming period:
Summer
Soil type:
Light, well-drained soil
Sun or Shade:
Prefers a warm sunny position
Hardiness:
Minimum temp 4°C (40°F)

Tagetes tenuifolia • *Signet Marigold*

Species, variety or cultivar:
'Starfire'
Other common names:
Signet Marigold, Striped Marigold
Height and spread:
80 x 60 cm (32 x 24 in)
Blooming period:
Summer to autumn
Soil type:
Light, well-drained soil
Sun or Shade:
Prefers a warm sunny position
Hardiness:
Minimum temp 4°C (40°F)

Description

T. tenuifolia is an annual found from Mexico to Colombia, and although sometimes narrowly upright, it is usually bushy, with fine branches. Many toothed pinnate leaves, with narrow lance-shaped segments, cover the plant, and abundant small, bright yellow, 5-petalled flowerheads with short ray florets, are borne from early summer through to autumn.

'Starfire' is a seedling mix, which comes in various shades of yellow, orange and red. Plant in a warm sunny position in a light, well-drained soil, and water well, making sure to feed if the foliage begins to yellow. Remove spent flowerheads regularly to prolong the flowering season.

Thunbergia alata • *Black-eyed Susan Vine*

Description

This is an Old World tropical genus from Africa and Asia, containing around 100 species of annuals, perennials and shrubs that are members of the acanthus (Acanthaceae) family. Flowers occur in a wide colour range, but most often yellow, orange and purple-blue shades, borne singly or in racemes and are generally long-tubed trumpets with five large lobes.

T. alata is a twining annual from tropical Africa, quick-growing with many long stems and heart-shaped, toothed leaves. Its numerous flowers are usually orange with a near-black throat, but are sometimes cream to yellow and/or evenly coloured, and they are borne in early summer. This is an ideal plant for hanging baskets.

Species, variety or cultivar:
–
Other common names:
Black-eyed Susan Vine
Height and spread:
3 x 3 m (10 x 10 ft)
Blooming period:
Summer
Soil type:
Moist, humus-rich, well-drained soil
Sun or Shade:
Full or part sun
Hardiness:
Minimum temp –1°C (30°F)

Tithonia rotundifolia • *Mexican Sunflower*

DESCRIPTION

This genus of ten species of annuals, perennials and shrubs is native to Mexico and Central America and is a member of the daisy (Asteraceae) family. Quite shrubby species, they are robust plants, sometimes with hairy stems, and have alternate leaves that are often lobed. They bear large daisy flowers in shades of yellow and orangey scarlet.

T. rotundifolia is an annual from Mexico and Central America and is a rapidly forming, large, many-branched plant with velvety-hairy leaves, to 30 cm (12 in) long. Orange ray flowers with tufted yellow centres are borne from summer to autumn, or first frost. 'Torch' is an eye-catching cultivar, with orange-red flowers, and a contrasting yellow centre.

Tithonias are useful for providing a bright spot in late summer and autumn. Grow them in a well-drained, moderately fertile soil in full sun, and propagate from seed or cuttings.

FAR LEFT AND LEFT: With mostly sun and fertile soil the Mexican Sunflower can get absolutely huge. They can grow to nearly 2.3 m (8 ft) tall and need plenty of space. It is advisable to stake these plants to stop them from blowing over in the wind.

Species, variety or cultivar:
'Torch'

Other common names:
Black-eyed Susan Vine

Height and spread:
1.8 x 0.6 m (6 x 2 ft)

Blooming period:
Summer to autumn

Soil type:
Well-drained, moderately fertile soil

Sun or Shade:
Enjoys full sun

Hardiness:
Minimum temp –7°C (20°F)

Torenia fournieri • *Bluewings*

Description

A genus of up to 50 species from tropical parts of Africa and Asia, which are noted for their ability to bloom well in both shady and sunny conditions. *T. fournieri* is a small bushy species from tropical Asia with pale green lightly serrated leaves, 5 cm (2 in) long, forming mounds on stems. The flowers are pale purple, and generally appear from late spring and finish once the first frosts start. This species makes an excellent edging plant for beds, borders and shade or woodland gardens, as well as for containers or window boxes. The cultivar 'Blue Panda' has a compact habit with lilac blue flowers.

Species, variety or cultivar:
'Blue Panda'

Other common names:
Bluewings, Wishbone Flower

Height and spread:
30 x 25 cm (12 x 10 in)

Blooming period:
Spring to autumn

Soil type:
Consistently moist, organically rich, well-drained soils

Sun or Shade:
Part-shade to full sun

Hardiness:
Minimum temp 4°C (40°F)

Trachelium caeruleum • *Throatwort*

Species, variety or cultivar:
–
Other common names:
Throatwort
Height and spread:
90 x 45 cm (36 x 18 in)
Blooming period:
Summer
Soil type:
Reasonably fertile, well-drained soil
Sun or Shade:
Prefers a sunny position
Hardiness:
Minimum temp –7°C (20°F)

Description

A small genus of seven species of herbs belonging to the bellflower (Campanulaceae) family, is native to Mediterranean regions, and is usually found growing in rocky crevices. They range from tiny cushion-forming species to more robust, erect, woody-based plants. Their simple leaves are alternately arranged.

T. caeruleum, suitable for border planting, is the most commonly seen species, flowering from seed in its first year or grown as an annual. An upright plant from the Mediterranean, it has serrated-edged, pointed, oval leaves and rounded clusters of tiny, starry, pleasantly perfumed, purple flowers, borne in summer. Very long protruding styles give the flowerheads a soft fluffy appearance.

Trachelospermum jasminoides • *Star Jasmine*

Species, variety or cultivar:
'Tricolor'

Other common names:
Confederate Jasmine, Star Jasmine

Height and spread:
9 x 8 m (30 x 25 ft)

Blooming period:
Summer to autumn

Soil type:
Prefers well-drained situations with some organic matter soil

Sun or Shade:
Happy in both sun and shade

Hardiness:
Minimum temp –12°C (10°F)

Description

A genus of about 20 species of evergreen climbing and twining plants found originally in woodland areas from Japan to India, and part of the Dogbane (Apocynaceae) family. *T. jasminoides* is a twining climber from Korea, Japan and China, with oval to elliptical, dark green, glossy leaves, to 10 cm (4 in) long. Masses of very fragrant white flowers appear in clusters, in summer to mid-autumn. These plants are popular in the ornamental garden for covering fences and pergolas or to clamber up tree trunks, but can also be grown as a ground cover plant. 'Tricolor' is a very popular cultivar, with eye-catching red, yellow and green foliage.

Triticum aestivum • *Bread Wheat*

Species, variety or cultivar:
–
Other common names:
Bread Wheat
Height and spread:
1.5 x 0.5 m (60 x 20 in)
Blooming period:
Summer
Soil type:
Most soils
Sun or Shade:
Needs full sun
Hardiness:
Minimum temp –7°C (20°F)

Description

This genus of about 30 annual clumping grasses, originating from temperate regions of the Middle East and North Africa, is a member of the grass (Poaceae) family. The ripe seed heads of *T. aestivum*, the world's most important cereal crop, are used for making bread flour, and this species is found throughout the plains of the world wherever cereal crops are grown. Flat, rough, narrow, strap-like leaves adorn a smooth hollow stem, and flowers in dense, somewhat flattened, stalkless spikelets, are borne in summer. Bearded seed heads of oval-shaped kernels, most commonly yellowish brown, also red, white, purple or blue are ground to create the flour used to make cereals and bread.

Tropaeolum majus • *Nasturtium*

Species, variety or cultivar:
–
Other common names:
Nasturtium
Height and spread:
3 x 3 m (10 x 10 ft)
Blooming period:
Summer
Soil type:
Moist, well-drained soil
Sun or Shade:
Likes both full and part sun
Hardiness:
Minimum temp –7°C (20°F)

Description

T. majus is an annual climber or scrambler found from Colombia to Bolivia, which has near round, sometimes shallowly lobed, dull green leaves. Flowers to over 5 cm (2 in) wide, long-spurred and 5-petalled, in shades of yellow, orange and red, are borne in summer. The species is now grown mainly in the form of seed-raised cultivars in various colours, some of which are double-flowered. It is possible that some cultivars are of hybrid origin, with other annual species such as *T. minus* and *T. peltophorum* in their parentage, but breeders have not revealed their history.

Tropaeolum majus • *Nasturtium*

Species, variety or cultivar:
Gleam Hybrid, 'Gleaming Lemons'
Other common names:
Nasturtium
Height and spread:
3 x 3 m (10 x 10 ft)
Blooming period:
Summer
Soil type:
Moist, well-drained soil
Sun or Shade:
Enjoys both full and part sun
Hardiness:
Minimum temp –7°C (20°F)

Description

This genus of over 80 species of sometimes tuberous annuals and perennials is found from southern Mexico to the southern tip of South America. The name comes from the Greek *tropaion*, 'trophy', a term used for the tree trunk on which were hung the shields and helmets of defeated enemies.

T. majus is found from Colombia to Bolivia, and long-spurred 5-petalled flowers to over 5 cm (2 in) wide, which appear in shades of yellow, orange and red, in summer. Gleam Hybrids come in either mixed colours or individual colours, such as 'Gleaming Lemons', which is a rich golden yellow.

Tropaeolum majus • *Nasturtium*

Description

The type genus for the nasturtium (Tropaeolaceae) family, this group of over 80 species of sometimes tuberous annuals and perennials, is found from southern Mexico to the southern tip of South America. Many climb using their twining leaf stalks. Though variable, the foliage is often shield-shaped and tinted blue-green. All have long-spurred 5-petalled flowers in a wide range of mainly warm shades.

T. majus, an annual climber or scrambler found from Colombia to Bolivia, has near round, sometimes shallowly lobed, dull green leaves, and flowers to over 5 cm (2 in) wide. Long-spurred and 5-petalled, these blooms appear in shades of yellow, orange and red, in summer. The species is now grown mainly in the form of seed-raised cultivars in various colours, some of which are double-flowered. The Whirlibird Series is low and spreading, and flowers in most colours, such as 'Whirlibird Cherry Rose', which has attractive dark pink blooms.

BELOW: Peach Melba 'Superior Wina'. If you nibble on a nasturtium leaf you will notice that it has a hot, peppery taste. The ancient Roman author Pliny is often quoted as stating that its spiciness gave nasturtium its name of 'nose twister' (Latin *nas-* 'nose' + *tor[que]mentum* 'twisted').

Species, variety or cultivar:
Whirlibird Series, 'Whirlibird Cherry Rose'

Other common names:
Nasturtium

Height and spread:
3 x 3 m (10 x 10 ft)

Blooming period:
Summer

Soil type:
Moist, well-drained soil

Sun or Shade:
Likes both full and part sun

Hardiness:
Minimum temp –7°C (20°F)

Tweedia caerulea • *Tweedia*

Species, variety or cultivar:
'Heaven Bow'
Other common names:
Tweedia
Height and spread:
90 x 90 cm (36 x 36 in)
Blooming period:
Summer
Soil type:
Well-drained, moderately fertile soil
Sun or Shade:
Prefers full sun
Hardiness:
Minimum temp –1°C (30°F)

Description

This genus, which is a member of the milkweed (Asclepiadaceae) family, contains a single species of twining or scrambling shrub, native to subtropical South America. It is sparsely branched with softly hairy stems and foliage. The oblong to heart-shaped leaves are up to 25 cm (10 in) long and the starry pale blue flowers are borne in summer and autumn. They are long-lasting when cut.

A twining or scrambling shrub, native to southern Brazil and Uruguay. It has lightly hairy greyish-green leaves. Its flowers are starry pale blue, which darken to lilac as they age, for long periods from summer. 'Heaven Bow', has pretty pale blue to lilac flowers, which look almost painted.

Verbena, hybrid cultivar • *Vervain*

DESCRIPTION

There are 250 species of annuals, perennials and subshrubs in this genus, native to tropical and subtropical America. The plants are sprawling to erect, usually with square, sometimes hairy, stems. Leaves are opposite and variously divided.

Among the many hybrid groups is the Quartz Series, characterized by a spreading, mounding habit, and large inflorescences of florets held above the foliage. This series does well in cool climates, tolerating light frosts, and is resistant to mildew. The award winning 'Quartz Burgundy' is a dwarf form suited to containers, and has deep wine red flowers with tiny white eyes that flower for an extended period.

Species, variety or cultivar:
Quartz Series, 'Quartz Burgundy'

Other common names:
Vervain, Garden Verbena

Height and spread:
20 x 37 cm (8 x 15 in)

Blooming period:
Summer to autumn

Soil type:
Moderately fertile moist, but well-drained soil

Sun or Shade:
Enjoys full sun

Hardiness:
Minimum temp –18°C (0°F)

Verbena, hybrid cultivar • *Vervain*

Description

This member of the self-named vervain (Verbenaceae) family contains 250 species of annuals, perennials and subshrubs native to tropical and subtropical America. The plants are sprawling to erect, usually with square, sometimes hairy, stems. Leaves are opposite and variously divided. The terminal flowerheads range from narrow and overlapping to broader, rounder clusters. Individual flowers are tubular with flaring, sometimes notched, lobes. Flowers come in shades of purple, pink, red and white.

Among the many hybrid groups is the Quartz Series, characterized by a spreading, mounding habit, and large inflorescences of florets held above the foliage. This series does well in cool climates, tolerating light frosts, and is resistant to mildew. 'Quartz Scarlet' has vigorous, scarlet flowers. Grow in the border in full sun in moderately fertile, moist but well-drained soil. Space plants about 28 cm (10 in) apart, and keep the soil moderately moist. Feed monthly with a balanced liquid fertilizer.

Species, variety or cultivar:
Quartz Series, 'Quartz Scarlet'

Other common names:
Vervain, Garden Verbena

Height and spread:
8 x 15 in. (20 x 37 cm)

Blooming period:
Summer to autumn

Soil type:
Moderately fertile moist, but well-drained soil

Sun or Shade:
Likes full sun

Hardiness:
Minimum temp 0°F (–18°C)

LEFT AND ABOVE: The 'Quartz' series are excellent garden performers. They have a spreading, mounded growth habit and hold their flowers well above the foliage. The brightly coloured flowers of Verbena are excellent for attracting Butterflies. Other colours that are available in this series are: Blue (the only Blue Verbena), Burgundy, Rose Scarlet, White, Polka Dot Mix and Quartz Mix.

Verbena, hybrid cultivar • *Vervain*

DESCRIPTION

This genus, a member of the vervain (Verbenaceae) family, contains 250 species of annuals, perennials and subshrubs native to tropical and subtropical America. The plants are sprawling to erect, usually with square, sometimes hairy, stems, and leaves that are opposite and variously divided. The terminal flowerheads range from narrow and overlapping to broader, rounder clusters. Individual flowers are tubular with flaring, sometimes notched, lobes.

The Tapien Series is comprised of low-growing, dense, long-flowering forms with fine foliage, that come in a variety of shades ranging from pink, through lavender, to blue. They thrive in hot summer weather and cope well in drought conditions. For an abundant flowering ground cover, plant around 45 cm (18 in) apart in spring, and expect blooms from summer through to autumn. 'Tapien Blue' has masses of flowers that are actually more magenta or purple than blue. As well as a great ground cover, this plant is also ideal for rockeries or containers, which can accentuate the cascading blooms.

BELOW: *Verbena tapiens* is an outstanding series of hybrids with dark green finely cut foliage and strongly prostrate habits. Flowers range from dark purple through red, rose pink, salmon pink, soft pink, light lavender and pale blue. They are great in hanging baskets, and will take to trimming well, responding with thickened habit and renewed flowering.

Species, variety or cultivar:
Tapien Series, 'Tapien Blue'

Other common names:
Vervain, Garden Verbena

Height and spread:
10 x 45 cm (4 x 18 in)

Blooming period:
Summer to autumn

Soil type:
Moderately fertile moist, but well-drained soil

Sun or Shade:
Prefers full sun

Hardiness:
Minimum temp –18°C (0°F)

Verbena, hybrid cultivar • *Vervain*

Species, variety or cultivar:
Tapien Series, 'Tapien Lavender'

Other common names:
Vervain, Garden Verbena

Height and spread:
60 x 100 cm (24 x 40 in)

Blooming period:
Summer to autumn

Soil type:
Moderately fertile moist, but well-drained soil

Sun or Shade:
Needs full sun

Hardiness:
Minimum temp –18°C (0°F)

Description

Verbenas are sprawling to erect, usually with square, sometimes hairy, stems, and leaves that are opposite and variously divided. Terminal flowerheads range from narrow and overlapping to broader, rounder clusters, and individual flowers are tubular with flaring, sometimes notched, lobes, in shades of purple, pink, red and white.

The Tapien Series is comprised of low-growing, long-flowering forms with fine foliage, flowering from summer to autumn in a variety of shades ranging from pink, through lavender, to blue. For an abundant flowering ground cover, plant around 45 cm (18 in) apart in spring. 'Tapien Lavender' has lilac to lavender 5-petalled flowers.

Verbena, hybrid cultivar • *Vervain*

Species, variety or cultivar:
Temari Series, 'Temari Patio Blue'

Other common names:
Vervain, Garden Verbena

Height and spread:
60 x 100 cm (24 x 40 in)

Blooming period:
Summer to autumn

Soil type:
Moderately fertile moist, but well-drained soil

Sun or Shade:
Enjoys full sun

Hardiness:
Minimum temp –18°C (0°F)

Description

The fragrant Temari Series is characterized by low-growing, trailing, fern-like foliage, which forms dense mats, and large, long-flowering blooms in shades of pink, burgundy, blue and scarlet. Members of this relatively recent series are vigorous growers, with some reaching over 90 cm (3 ft), and the series has larger leaves than the fine foliage of the Tapien Series. 'Temari Patio Blue' is an upright bushy plant with large numbers of attractive purple flower clusters being borne from early summer through to autumn. The rich colour of the blooms, and their tendency to spill over the top of containers, makes this an ideal choice for a patio plant, as the name would suggest.

Verbena, hybrid cultivar • *Vervain*

Description

There are 250 species of annuals, perennials and subshrubs native to tropical and subtropical America in this genus. Individual flowers are tubular with flaring, sometimes notched, lobes, and come in shades of purple, pink, red and white. The common name vervain comes from the Celtic ferfaen, 'to drive away a stone', a reference to the use of *V. officinalis* as a cure for bladder infections. It was also a supposed aphrodisiac and cure-all for problems ranging from snakebites to heart disease.

The vigorous Temari Series is characterized by low-growing, trailing, fern-like foliage, which forms dense mats, and large long-flowering blooms in a variety of colours. A fast-spreading plant, 'Temari Burgundy' has deep wine-red to magenta flowers and velvety petals, thrives in heat and full sun, and resists powdery mildew. Temari means 'flower ball' in Japanese, and describes how the plant blooms in large clusters of flowers. Grow in full sun in moderately fertile, moist but well-drained soil.

LEFT AND BELOW: This series spreads fast forming a dense mat covered with large flowerheads in a wide variety of colours. Very heat and cold tolerant and resistant to powdery mildew this is a great choice for pots, baskets or any planting in full sun.

Species, variety or cultivar:
Temari Series, 'Temari Burgundy'

Other common names:
Vervain, Garden Verbena

Height and spread:
60 x 100 cm (24 x 40 in)

Blooming period:
Summer to autumn

Soil type:
Moderately fertile moist, but well-drained soil

Sun or Shade:
Likes full sun

Hardiness:
Minimum temp –18°C (0°F)

Verbena, hybrid cultivar • *Vervain*

Species, variety or cultivar:
Temari Series, 'Temari Scarlet'

Other common names:
Vervain, Garden Verbena

Height and spread:
60 x 100 cm (24 x 40 in)

Blooming period:
Summer to autumn

Soil type:
Moderately fertile moist, but well-drained soil

Sun or Shade:
Prefers full sun

Hardiness:
Minimum temp –18°C (0°F)

Description

Vigorous and fragrant, the Temari Series is typified by low-growing, trailing, fern-like foliage, which forms dense mats, and large long-flowering variously-coloured blooms. Members of this relatively recent series are fast-spreading, and some can reach over 90 cm (3 ft) in height. The rich colour of the blooms, and their tendency to spill over the top of containers, makes this an ideal choice for a patio plant, as the name would suggest. Grow in full sun in moderately fertile, moist but well-drained soil. 'Temari Scarlet', probably the most popular hanging basket variety of verbena, has multiple scarlet-coloured flowerheads up to 5 cm (2 in) across borne on trailing stems.

Viola, hybrid cultivar • *Pansy*

Species, variety or cultivar:
Crystal Bowl Series, 'Crystal Bowl Orange'

Other common names:
Pansy, Viola

Height and spread:
30 x 40 cm (12 x 16 in)

Blooming period:
Spring to summer

Soil type:
Moist, well-drained soil

Sun or Shade:
Does best in full or part sun

Hardiness:
Minimum temp –18°C (0°F)

Description

The Crystal Bowl Series is just one of the many Viola series. The members of the Crystal Bowl Series feature 5-petalled flowers in a range of eye-catching bright colours. They are compact clump-forming plants that exhibit good tolerance to heat. The dark green leaves serve as a contrast to the pure colours of the mid- to large sized flowers. Crystal Bowl Series cultivars make ideal bedding or container plants, bringing a blaze of colour to the garden. The flowers of 'Crystal Bowl Orange' feature five large golden orange petals fanned out around a small yellow centre.

Viola, hybrid cultivar • *Pansy*

Description

With more than 500 species and many cultivars to its name, the Viola genus offers a wealth of choice for growing conditions. Violas are a popular selection for bedding, for container planting, for hanging baskets, or for the rock garden. The many hybrids available are annuals or short-lived perennials developed from *V. cornuta, V. corsica* and *V. tricolor*, and other mainly European species. These compact plants have fleshy dark green leaves, measuring up to 5 cm (2 in) long, which are shallowly lobed.

The Crystal Bowl Series of large pure-coloured cultivars includes 'Crystal Bowl True Blue'. As its name suggests, this cultivar displays a whorl of five clear blue petals around a tiny bright yellow eye. Though it prefers a shady location, this plant offers a reasonable tolerance to heat, and a fairly long flowering season, provided any spent flowers are removed before the plant sets seeds.

Species, variety or cultivar:
Crystal Bowl Series, 'Crystal Bowl True Blue'

Other common names:
Pansy, Viola

Height and spread:
30 x 40 cm (12 x 16 in)

Blooming period:
Spring to summer

Soil type:
Moist, well-drained soil

Sun or Shade:
Enjoys full or part sun

Hardiness:
Minimum temp –18°C (0°F)

Viola, hybrid cultivar • *Pansy*

Species, variety or cultivar:
Imperial Series, 'Imperial Frosty Rose'

Other common names:
Pansy, Viola

Height and spread:
15 x 15 cm (6 x 6 in)

Blooming period:
Spring to summer

Soil type:
Moist, well-drained soil

Sun or Shade:
Easily grown in full or part sun

Hardiness:
Minimum temp −18°C (0°F)

Description

Viola species are found in all the world's temperate zones from the mountains of New Zealand to the subarctic. Featuring lush, elliptic, kidney- or heart-shaped leaves and 5-petalled flowers available in a spectrum of colours, Viola are the type genus for the family Violaceae.

The Imperial Series of cultivars display mid- to large sized flowers, chiefly in shades of dusky pink and apricot pastel shades. 'Imperial Frosty Rose' features lush, bright green leaves and attractive mid-sized flowers, with lower petals of dusky rose-purple fading to a softer, paler pink towards the petal edges, and lighter, almost white, upper petals.

Viola, hybrid cultivar • *Pansy*

Species, variety or cultivar:
Ultima Series, 'Ultima Baron Purple'

Other common names:
Pansy, Viola

Height and spread:
30 x 40 cm (12 x 16 in)

Blooming period:
Spring to summer

Soil type:
Moist, well-drained soil

Sun or Shade:
Enjoys full or part sun

Hardiness:
Minimum temp –18°C (0°F)

Description

Though there are some 500-odd species in the Viola genus, all violas have remarkably similarly shaped 5-petalled flowers, with the lower petal often carrying dark markings. White, yellow and purple predominate, but the flowers occur in every colour, at least among the garden forms.

A somewhat fast-growing selection, the cultivars of the Ultima Series are available in a wide range of colours. 'Ultima Baron Purple' displays petals with a rim of dark purple, edging a ring of purple-streaked golden yellow, which encircles the darker purple centre. At the centre of the bold mix of colours is a small yellow eye.

Viola, hybrid cultivar • *Pansy*

Description

The flowers of Viola hybrid cultivars are variably sized from small to giant styles nearly 8 cm (3 in) wide, in virtually all colours, and many beautiful combinations and patterns. The fleshy leaves are pointed oval to lance-shaped. The Ultima Series cultivars are fast-growing, offering early and plentiful colour to the garden as they are among the early-blooming violas and are heavy flowering. The large flowers come in a wide colour range including single-coloured, blotched and pastel types, in shades of lavender, scarlet, yellow, bronze-apricot and pale salmon orange.

'Ultima Baron Red' presents a vibrant cheery face to the world, with its stunning combination of carmine and gold petals, with darker veining radiating outwards towards the petal edges. True to type, 'Ultima Baron Red' is an early flowering selection and a prolific flowerer. This compact plant is an ideal choice for spring or autumn planting, providing bright colour to borders or baskets.

LEFT AND BELOW: Violas are cool season plants, and this makes them ideal for high altitude gardens, as well as early and late season planting at lower elevations. Plant in any well-drained fertile soil in full sun to partial shade in either beds or containers.

Species, variety or cultivar:
Ultima Series, 'Ultima Baron Red'

Other common names:
Pansy, Viola

Height and spread:
30 x 40 cm (12 x 16 in)

Blooming period:
Spring to summer

Soil type:
Moist, well-drained soil

Sun or Shade:
Prefers full or part sun

Hardiness:
Minimum temp –18°C (0°F)

Viola, hybrid cultivar • *Pansy*

Species, variety or cultivar:
Velour Series, 'Velour Blue Bronze'
Other common names:
Pansy, Viola
Height and spread:
30 x 40 cm (12 x 16 in)
Blooming period:
Spring to summer
Soil type:
Moist, well-drained soil
Sun or Shade:
Does best in full or part sun
Hardiness:
Minimum temp –18°C (0°F)

Description

Popular around the world for the welcome spring colour they provide in the garden, violas come in a complete palette of colours. The garden hybrids offer an extensive choice of flower size, colour, flowering time and habit. Some cultivars have been developed to handle cooler climates than others, and some offer an earlier or longer flowering season.

The Velour Series plants have medium to large flowers, which come in intense shades, often with dark markings, and with an exotic velvet texture. 'Velour Blue Bronze' has a soft bronze lustre on the lower petals, contrasting with the upper petals of clear blue.

Viola tricolor • *Heartsease*

Description

Symbolically, *V. tricolor* was adopted by both the city of Athens and by Napoleon. Native to temperate Eurasia, *V. tricolor* can be annual, biennial or perennial – though it is most often treated as an annual. The shallowly lobed or toothed leaves are pointed oval to lance-shaped, while the small flowers are bi- or multi-coloured, often with face-like patterning. There are many cultivars and seedling strains of *V. tricolor*, including the striking 'Bowles' Black' (syn. 'E. A. Bowles'), with its intense black flowers, reaching up to 3 cm (1½ in) wide. These stunning flowers have a velvety texture, and feature a bright yellow centre.

Species, variety or cultivar:
'Bowles' Black'

Other common names:
Heartsease, Johnny Jump-Up, Love-in-Idleness

Height and spread:
35 x 40 cm (14 x 16 in)

Blooming period:
Spring to early summer

Soil type:
Moist, well-drained soil

Sun or Shade:
Suitable for full sun to shade

Hardiness:
Minimum temp –34°C (–30°F)

Viola, hybrid cultivar • *Pansy*

Description

A large genus, Viola is an old-fashioned favourite and a popular choice with gardeners. The genus contains many species with a history of use – medicinally, symbolically and as a food source. A number of series are included in the hybrid cultivars, each with distinctive qualities. With their vast selection of bold colours, violas lend themselves perfectly to colour-themed gardens. Their low-growing habit makes them ideal candidates not only for accentuating the front of borders, but also for drawing attention to the entire bed. Time spent maintaining these plants, in conjunction with removal of dead flowers, can often reward with a second season of flowers.

Boldly patterned mid-sized flowers, usually combining blue and another colour, are the trademark of the Joker Series. 'Joker Poker Face' produces impressive flowers of rich purple and gold. The upper petals are intense purple, while the lower petals feature bright gold 'ink-blot' patterning on the velvety purple template.

BELOW: Jolly Joker is probably the most spectacular pansy of its class. The intense orange of its lower petals, contrasts sharply with the deep purple of the upper petals. The effect is both unusual and intriguing. A very versatile and hardy variety which can be sown early for summer flowers or in summer for flowering in autumn and spring, and even, in mild winters, through the winter.

Species, variety or cultivar:
Joker Series, 'Joker Poker Face'

Other common names:
Pansy, Viola

Height and spread:
30 x 40 cm (12 x 16 in)

Blooming period:
Spring to early summer

Soil type:
Moist, well-drained soil

Sun or Shade:
Prefers full or part sun

Hardiness:
Minimum temp –18°C (0°F)

Zaluzianskya ovata

Description

This genus in the foxglove (Scrophulariaceae) family consists of about 35 species of sticky-leafed annuals, perennials and subshrubs from southern and eastern Africa. Their leaves are smooth or toothed and the flowers have five spreading notched petals at the end of a long tube. Most are night-scented and the outside colour of the flowers is quite different from the inside. The genus is named after Adam Zaluziansky von Zaluzian, a sixteenth-century Bohemian botanist.

Z. ovata is a brittle-stemmed species from South Africa, with toothed leaves to 4 cm (1¾ in) long. Flowers are white inside with rich crimson on the petal backs, produced over a long period in summer–autumn. This species like full sun and a well-drained soil in almost frost-free climates. Where frost is usual, they can be grown in a cool greenhouse as a colourful filler. Take tip cuttings in summer or sow seed in spring with bottom heat, and keep almost dry in winter.

Species, variety or cultivar:
–

Other common names:
–

Height and spread:
25 x 60 cm (10 x 24 in)

Blooming period:
Summer to autumn

Soil type:
Well-drained soil

Sun or Shade:
Needs full sun

Hardiness:
Minimum temp –1°C (30°F)

Zea mays • *Maize*

Species, variety or cultivar:
'Blue Jade'
Other common names:
Corn, Maize, Mealie, Indian Corn, Sweet Corn
Height and spread:
4.5 x 1 m (15 x 3 ft)
Blooming period:
Summer
Soil type:
Most soil types
Sun or Shade:
Needs an open position in full sun
Hardiness:
Minimum temp –12°C (10°F)

Description

This genus of four annual grasses, members of the grass (Poaceae) family, is native to Central America, with strong upright stems and broad, smooth, strap-like leaves. Male flowers are at the tops of stems, while female flowers grow from the leaf axils, with a solid core enclosed within the leaves in summer. Fruit forms as massed grains around the core in late summer–autumn.

Z. mays, which is high in nutritional value, is widely grown as a food crop for humans and to fatten cattle. Ornamental cultivars are also available. 'Blue Jade' is a dwarf with a bushy habit, and deep bluish black kernels.

Zea mays • *Maize*

DESCRIPTION

Originally from Central America, *Z. mays* is now widely grown worldwide as a food crop, and has upright, stout, robust stems and smooth strap-like leaves, to 90 cm (36 in) long, in two ranks, with pointed tips and sheathed bases. Feathery male flowers grow in terminal panicles, while female flowers are borne in heads to 20 cm (8 in) long, growing from leaf axils, and are packed with shining, yellow, white or black grains, to 1 cm (2/5 in) across, enclosed within leaves. When people think of corn, they picture something like the cultivar 'New Excellence', which has sweet yellow kernels.

Species, variety or cultivar:
'New Excellence'

Other common names:
Corn, Maize, Mealie, Indian Corn, Sweet Corn

Height and spread:
4.5 x 1 m (15 x 3 ft)

Blooming period:
Summer

Soil type:
Most soil types

Sun or Shade:
Needs an open sunny position

Hardiness:
Minimum temp –12°C (10°F)

Zinnia angustifolia

Description

Z. angustifolia is an erect summer-flowering annual. Its natural distribution ranges from southeastern USA to Mexico. It has needle-like to narrow lance-shaped leaves, which reach up to 8 cm (3 in) long. The flowerheads feature up to nine bright orange ray florets and orange disc florets, which are interspersed with dark hairs. For best results, plant zinnias in a sheltered spot where they will be protected from draughts. While they prefer moist well-drained soils, they can withstand dry periods, and adapt well to rock garden planting. Removing spent flowers regularly will extend the flowering season of these popular garden plants. They also make excellent cut flower subjects for indoor floral displays, and should be cut just before the flower opens.

There are several selected forms, including 'Coral Beauty', which can reach up to 30 cm (12 in) high. This heat tolerant cultivar bears attractive, semi-double, bright coral-coloured blooms.

Species, variety or cultivar:
'Coral Beauty'

Other common names:
–

Height and spread:
12 x 20 in. (30 x 50 cm)

Blooming period:
Summer

Soil type:
Moist, well-drained soil

Sun or Shade:
Likes a sunny warm position

Hardiness:
Minimum temp 20°F (–7°C)

LEFT: *Zinnia angustifolia* 'Crystal White'

Zinnia elegans

Description

Zinnia, a member of the daisy (Asteraceae) family, is a genus of around 20 species of annuals, perennials and small shrubs. Their natural distribution extends from south-central USA to Argentina, with its centre in Mexico. Enjoying hot dry conditions, these attractive plants are popular with gardeners for their colourful daisy-like flowers.

Z. elegans is a summer-flowering species that has produced many cultivars, which are available in an extensive range of colours. It has pointed oval to lance-shaped leaves, often with a fine cover of hairs. The cultivar 'Aztek' bears creamy white flowers, with its ray florets radiating around a central raised disc.

Species, variety or cultivar:
'Aztek'

Other common names:
–

Height and spread:
100 x 45 cm (40 x 18 in)

Blooming period:
Summer

Soil type:
Moist, well-drained soil

Sun or Shade:
Enjoys a sunny warm position

Hardiness:
Minimum temp –7°C (20°F)

Zinnia elegans

Description

Predominantly from Mexico, the two most prolific species of Zinnia are *Z. elegans* and *Z. haageana. Z. elegans,* in particular, has produced many cultivars, and there are a number of series available. Retaining the general characteristics of the species, each of these series brings a unique characteristic to the garden. In the case of the Mammoth Exhibition Series, the plants are among the tallest available, reaching a height of up to 75 cm (30 in). Producing the largest flowers of the genus, the giant double flowers in this series are available in a wide range of colours.

Species, variety or cultivar:
Mammoth Exhibition Series

Other common names:
–

Height and spread:
75 x 45 cm (30 x 18 in)

Blooming period:
Summer

Soil type:
Moist, well-drained soil

Sun or Shade:
Likes a warm position in full sun

Hardiness:
Minimum temp –7°C (20°F)

Zinnia elegans

DESCRIPTION

Zinnias are among the most popular garden flowers, introducing bold vibrant colours to the garden. The cultivated plants are mostly frost-tender summer annuals, and they should be grown in a sunny warm position, sheltered from draughts. While the flowers of the wild species are typically daisy-like with conspicuous ray and disc florets, modern seed strains are mainly doubles with the disc florets largely hidden or absent.

Among the many series of cultivars of *Z. elegans*, is the Profusion Series. This series produces single flowers in shades of red, orange or white. 'Profusion Cherry' has rich cherry-red ray florets around a golden central disc.

Species, variety or cultivar:
Profusion Series, 'Profusion Cherry'

Other common names:
–

Height and spread:
30 x 30 cm (12 x 12 in)

Blooming period:
Summer

Soil type:
Moist, well-drained soil

Sun or Shade:
Prefers a warm position in full sun

Hardiness:
Minimum temp –7°C (20°F)

Zinnia elegans

Description

Named for Johann Gottfried Zinn (1727–1759), a botany professor at Göttingen University, Germany, the Zinnia genus is perhaps best known for *Z. elegans* and its many cultivars. This species features soft light green leaves and daisy-like flowers. The colour range is very wide, though mostly confined to the warm tones: yellow, pink, orange and red to mahogany. Zinnias can be propagated easily from seed.

The Ruffles Series of cultivars produces double flowers, which are available in most colours. 'Pink Ruffles' features layers of soft pink ray florets radiating from a central disc floret of golden yellow.

Species, variety or cultivar:
Ruffles Series, 'Pink Ruffles'

Other common names:
–

Height and spread:
70 x 45 cm (27 x 18 in)

Blooming period:
Summer

Soil type:
Moist, well-drained soil

Sun or Shade:
Needs full sun

Hardiness:
Minimum temp –7°C (20°F)

Zinnia haageana • *Mexican Zinnia*

Description

An erect to broad and bushy summer-flowering annual, *Z. haageana* hails from Mexico, and is sometimes referred to as Mexican zinnia. The narrow, lance-shaped leaves are sparsely hairy to downy, and can measure over 3 cm (1¼ in) long. Held on tall stems, up to 30 cm (12 in) in height, the flowerheads feature eight to nine golden to red-brown ray florets around an orange disc, each flower measuring around 5 cm (2 in) across. A traditional favourite in gardens for bedding and borders, this species can tolerate hot dry conditions. As a general rule they should be watered regularly, though the plants should be well watered when initially planted in. These striking plants will also attract winged visitors to the garden, being favourites with bees, birds and butterflies.

Many cultivars have been developed from *Z. haageana*, and the fully double-flowered forms are common in cultivation. The cultivar 'Stargold' bears attractive yellow-orange flowers.

LEFT: Zinnia haageana 'Star White'

Species, variety or cultivar:
'Stargold'
Other common names:
Mexican Zinnia
Height and spread:
30 x 60 cm (12 x 24 in)
Blooming period:
Summer
Soil type:
Moist, well-drained soil
Sun or Shade:
Likes full sun in a warm position
Hardiness:
Minimum temp –7°C (20°F)

Zinnia peruviana • *Madagascar Periwinkle*

Species, variety or cultivar:
'Yellow Peruvian'
Other common names:
Madagascar Periwinkle, Periwinkle, Rosy Periwinkle
Height and spread:
90 x 40 cm (36 x 16 in)
Blooming period:
Summer
Soil type:
Moist, well-drained soil
Sun or Shade:
Enjoys a warm position in full sun
Hardiness:
Minimum temp –7°C (20°F)

Description

Z. peruviana is a fast-growing summer-flowering annual found from southern USA to Argentina. The narrow, bright green, lance-shaped leaves, can measure nearly 8 cm (3 in) long. Each of the flowerheads, which are borne on broad stems held clear above the foliage, have up to 15 red, dusky tangerine or yellow ray florets, up to 2.5 cm (1 in) long, around a yellow to purple-black disc. Exhibiting a tolerance for a wide range of conditions, this species can be invasive, so care should be taken when choosing a site for planting. The cultivar 'Yellow Peruvian' has yellow flowerheads that age to gold.

Index *of Latin names*

Index *of Common names*

Credits

Text and photographs by arrangement with Global Book Publishing Pty LTD.